Modernities

This book is dedicated to
Holly, Colette and Christian

Modernities

A Geohistorical Interpretation

Peter J. Taylor

Polity Press

First published in 1999 by Polity Press
in association with Blackwell Publishers Ltd.

Editorial office:
Polity Press
65 Bridge Street
Cambridge CB2 1UR, UK

Marketing and production:
Blackwell Publishers Ltd
108 Cowley Road
Oxford OX4 1JF, UK

ISBN 0-7456-2129-5
ISBN 0-7456-2130-9 (pbk)

A catalogue record for this book is available from the British Library.

Typeset in 11 on 13 pt Sabon
by Ace Filmsetting Ltd, Frome, Somerset
Printed in Great Britain by MPG Books Ltd, Bodmin, Cornwall

This book is printed on acid-free paper.

Contents

Contents

Epilogue: Presents and Ends

Preface

As a British resident, I will always remember 1997 as the year of the modern. In May a General Election landslide produced a New Labour government committed to modernizing Britain. It was led by people who called themselves modernizers. In August Diana, Princess of Wales, died and was immediately converted into a modern icon. Suddenly the words modern, modernity and modernization seemed to be on every news report. The Queen even complained about the world moving too fast, the time-honoured lament about living in a modern world. 1997 was a very modern year.

I had been thinking about modernity for some time before 1997. I began a project about world hegemony in 1990 and somewhere along the way this got interwoven with the concept of modernity. The result, in 1996, was *The Way the Modern World Works* (1996a), which some reviewers, tired of more about hegemony, had hoped contained rather more on modernity. In fact I only really begin to get to grips with modernity in the last chapter of the aforementioned book. This book builds upon *The Way* by restating the hegemony–modernity link (to make this book freestanding) but then takes it much further by adding some earlier work on modern politics and recent work and ideas on the ambiguity of modernization. In particular I use the book to promote what I term a geohistorical approach to social science as a reaction against some of the more esoteric treatments of its subject matter. The latter, after all, consists largely of the everyday experience of ordinary men and women.

This is my first book since moving to Loughborough University. I am relishing being in a department with so many fine researchers all interested, in their different ways, in the cultural-political-historical-global mix of ideas that fascinate me. I would defy any human geography researcher not to enjoy the collective intellectual stimulation provided by a group such as Jon Beaverstock, Morag Bell, Ed Brown, Marcus Doel, Mike Heffernan, Sarah Holloway, David Slater and David Walker. In addition, outside the department, there are leading social scientists such as Michael Billig, Linda Hantrais, Ruth Lister, Mike Smith and Robert Walker. Loughborough is a very good environment in which to pursue social science.

At the same time that I moved to Loughborough I became a granddad, a much more important transition in life. This book is dedicated to three bairns for their lovely smiles and impish grins and everything which goes with both.

Peter Taylor

Prologue: Being Geohistorical

Do you think of yourself as being modern? The chances are you will not have to think too hard about this question; instinctively most readers would say 'yes, of course I am modern'. To be modern is perceived as being essentially positive, it is about 'moving with the times', being up to date, following the latest fashions or using the newest gadgets. For the whole of the twentieth century and for some time before, many, many millions of people have subscribed to the idea of being modern or have aspired to becoming modern. At times modern appears to be an all-pervasive identity, ubiquitous and therefore taken for granted and, if not yet universal, destined to become so. Modern is what we are.

The hold that the idea of being modern has on contemporary life can be appreciated by considering the use of the word modern as an adjective. In my teaching I ask students to fill in the blank in the following: 'modern ....'. The range of suggestions is always extraordinary in its breadth. As well as well-known items such as modern jazz and modern art, this word association exercise penetrates all realms of social activity: modern furniture, modern ideas, modern industry, modern science, modern medicine, modern transport, modern families, modern fashion, modern marriages, modern country, modern warfare, modern shopping centres, modern homes, modern farming, modern diseases, modern technology, and the list goes on and on. In nearly all cases the word modern is being used to convey the idea that what is modern is better than what went before – Henri Lefebvre (1995, p. 185) calls it 'a prestigious word'. Advertisers, and politicians, know this association only too well. Academics are not immune to the attractiveness of this seductively simple adjective either: in one bibliographic search for 1990 to 1997 I was able to find 5,057 items which had modern in their title. I should add immediately that I was not able to read all this work but I presume that in much of these writings modern was being used with its meaning taken for granted. That is to say, it was not interrogated as a concept or idea in the body of the text. So pervasive is this that it may even be the case in situations where such intellectual examination is the *raison d'être* of the publication. The *Cassell Dictionary of Modern Politics* (East and Joseph, 1994) is just such a case in point; there is no entry for modern. I guess the implication is that such an entry is unnecessary, everybody knows what modern is. Hence the book before you is redundant . . . er, well no, do not be too hasty, please read on.

Of course, there have been dissidents loath to accept this popular view of being modern. Whether self-ascribed as anti-modern, non-modern or post-modern, they have stepped back from the simple acceptance of the equation modern equals better to problematize what is so commonly accepted. The limiting case is Bruno Latour (1993), who doubts whether we have ever been modern. The latter is viewed as an artificial construct of modern disciplines 'purifying' in their discourses what have always been hybrid networks of social practices no different from the hybrid 'pre-modern' societies anthropologists write about. Although I accept that many such critiques have been immensely valuable by forcing us to view being modern in a new light, in this book I am writing from within rather than without the modern. In fact, from the geohistorical position I define below, I will argue that it is now impossible to write from outside the modern and therefore all such critiques are themselves inherently modern. This irony is made possible because one important feature of being modern is that it is a human condition which is especially inquiring about the world.

It follows that, despite its pervasive 'given-ness', there are still many examples of this investigative penchant being turned on the concept of modern from within. In such 'internal' critiques, being modern is viewed, in Anthony Giddens's (1990, p. 7) words, as 'a double-edged phenomenon'. As well as the familiar triumphs of being modern, there is a downside. In the list using modern as an adjective above, there are modern warfare and modern diseases, which are hardly to be recommended. To argue that nuclear bombs are better than bows and arrows is to reveal a rather perverse sense of values. Obviously in any war situation modern weapons will prevail over past weaponry and are therefore 'better' but only in a very narrow sense. Unfortunately it seems that often the modern does define actions within a narrow instrumental mode of thinking which can easily lead to better at being bad. The Holocaust is the example where several aspects of being modern came together to create a horrific outcome. Although often interpreted as a primeval throwback to some past pre-modern condition, in reality this was a modern politics directing a modern bureaucracy which designed a modern organization combining modern transport, modern machinery and modern chemistry (Bauman, 1989). Evidently, modern has encompassed mass execution chambers as well as the latest designer clothes.

The purpose of this book is neither to celebrate nor to condemn being modern. Rather, I take a critical stance from a particular and, I think, undervalued perspective which I call geohistorical. The study of being modern in its various forms – I discuss modernity, modernism and modernization in chapter 1 – has been undertaken in many different ways from rather esoteric philosophical treatises to fairly humdrum abstracted empiricism which purports to measure being modern. All such studies may be considered as laying along a continuum with ahistorical-ageographical analyses at one end and geohistorical studies at the other. Studies at the pole opposite to my approach carefully delineate the meaning of modernity and then apply the definition as if it were independent of history and geography. For instance, Matthew Arnold in the 1860s outlined a timeless view of modernity by emphasizing particular intellectual and civic virtues focusing on a rationality he thought existed in Victorian England. Since he identified these same virtues in classical Athens, he designated the latter to be a modern society. Similarly, Baudelaire in the Paris of the 1850s, by focusing on the aesthetic, was able to argue that every age has its modernity represented by the painter capturing the fleeting and transitory in his work. In complete contrast, here I take a much more grounded and concrete view of being and becoming modern. If being modern is a taken-for-granted feature of life this implies it is embedded in everyday thinking and behaviour. Such a condition I shall term modernity. A geohistorical approach respects this embeddedness, never neglecting the contexts in which modern behaviour and thinking take place. Quite simply, embedding occurs in real time and space locations which are constitutive of the modernity under study. Hence a geohistorical interpretation of modernity is concerned to understand the specific periods and places where ideas and practices of being modern are created, challenged and changed.

Most studies of being modern fall between these two poles. Periods and places of creation and reproduction of modernity remain part of the analysis but they are less central, often, for instance, being relegated to an illustrative role. At its worst this can lead to a relatively random ransacking of history and geography to find suitable examples to prove a point. Even in more sensitive arguments, for instance using case studies for comparative analyses, period and place may be brought back into the analysis as context but the wider time–space structure will still be missing. In a geohistorical approach periods and places are not simply 'used', they are interpreted as being the concrete face of modernity as a single interconnected story and map. It is this combined story-and-map which identifies a geohistorical methodology.

There can be many such geohistories, of course, and here I develop one particular version which produces a few surprises to counter some assumptions many of the more abstract studies take for granted. In this prologue both the universal pretensions of modernity and the beneficiaries of modernity are brought under the spotlight to provide a taster of such surprises. I use a phonetic play on words, first 'who's modern?' and then 'whose modern?', to highlight the way in which a geohistorical approach forces certain questions to the fore.

Who's modern?

Some years ago, the question 'who is modern?' was asked by A. Inkeles and D. H. Smith (1974) in a major study of modernization in six third world countries. Arguing that development requires individuals to acquire the relevant attitudes and skills, to be 'modern man' (p. 5) as they term it, a standard sociological methodology was employed to answer the question. At the centre of the research was a questionnaire designed to measure the twelve personal qualities identified by the authors as making an individual effective in modern society. Surveying a large sample in each country, Inkeles and Smith were able to produce a score for every respondent on a 'composite scale' from 1 to 100. By aggregating these scores, the countries were ranked in terms of how rapidly they might become thoroughly modern like first world countries. Modernization studies such as this one have been properly criticized on many counts (see chapter 1), but they do raise an interesting question even if their answers are seen now as crude and simplistic.

Inkeles and Smith's study takes what I would call a liberal approach to defining modern. It is something individuals possess and therefore can be measured person by person. In the process every individual is abstracted out of her or his social context and tested by a universal measure. There is no sense of modernity as a geohistorical phenomenon, a network of opportunities and constraints which vary by time and place. Rather, an individual attribute is measured without reference to the necessary social support which makes being modern possible or indeed meaningful. If being modern is thought of in these more societal terms, it must be queried whether the idea of 'percentage modern' has any credence. I will take the view that being modern is one of those all-or-nothing conditions: either you are or you are not. In this book modernity is considered to be a condition experienced by people who live in a modern society; hence all such people are deemed to be modern by definition. Of course, this then begs the further question: what is a modern society?

Consider the following three people. It is the mid-eighteenth century and midway across the middle Atlantic a young African woman is in irons below deck in a slave ship. Captured in a minor war skirmish in her west African homeland she is destined, if she survives this journey, for Trinidad where she will be sold probably as a field hand in the sugar plantations. Moving on a century, it is the mid-nineteenth century and midway across central Ireland a small bedraggled family group is walking slowly in the direction of

Dublin. The young Irish woman in the group is appallingly thin, the result of famine since the potato blight hit her community the previous year. Leaving that behind, if she can survive to Dublin by foraging, she has vague hopes of reaching Liverpool or even the USA but with little knowledge of what to expect. Another century on and it is the mid-twentieth century and a young Thai woman is being driven in a Transit van, with others, to Bangkok by her new 'guardians'. Overburdened by debt, her peasant father has agreed to a payment in return for his eldest daughter going to work in the city. She faces a future of prostitution servicing American soldiers and Japanese tourists.

Are these three women modern? The initial reaction is to think not – certainly their stories as forced migrants are as old as humanity; the bible, for instance, has many references to slavery, famines and prostitution. Of even greater weight in drawing this first conclusion is the utter powerlessness of the women. The popular positive image of being modern does not seem to have room for victims. But what about those responsible for creating the women's dire circumstances, slavers, landlords and pimps? Again there is nothing particularly new in their roles, hence wielding power certainly does not automatically bequeath a modern status. Notice that this line of argument is related to the liberal interpretation of being modern I have criticized earlier. It is not individual roles that matter; rather, it is the overall context in which the roles are performed. The question can now be reformed: do our African, Irish and Thai women separated by the centuries nevertheless belong to a single story-and-map which can be identified as modern?

Returning to the concept of modern society, identifying such entities seems to be an easy task. American society, German society, Australian society and Japanese society, it would generally be agreed, are four of many examples which could be listed as modern societies. One commonly overlooked feature of such a list is the fact that these societies are politically bounded; each society corresponds geographically to a single state. There seems to be little theoretical justification for this society/state congruence, it is simply part of the contemporary taken-for-granted interpretation of the social world (Wallerstein, 1984). There is a simple geohistorical critique of such common thinking. If indeed societies are defined by states then they become as unstable as the states which contain them. For instance, there was an Estonian state created after World War I but destroyed in World War II; was there, therefore, also an Estonian society in the 1920s and 1930s which disappeared into Soviet society for half a century only to emerge again in the 1990s with the demise of the USSR and the recreation of an independent Estonia? Similarly, where there was one Yugoslav society just a decade ago, presumably there are now five societies to match the political division of the original state. Of course, such definitional problems are not merely a feature of the rise and fall of communist states. What about former states which are not on today's world political map; do their societies automatically vanish with them? For instance, did Newfoundland society disappear when the country became a province of Canada? For the counter case, consider Quebec: will a new society emerge only if the province wins independence? All of these examples suggest equating state and society is not a sensible thing to do. Society, as a much deeper social construction than politically created states, should be able to predate and outsurvive the political fact of a particular state's existence.

Equating society with state is a basically modern view of the world: the cartographic image of countries across the world forming a mosaic of bounded spaces is the most familiar of all maps. But this is very much a modern self-image we do not have to subscribe to. Globalization is an alternative vision of the world which is becoming increasingly popular. This is an argument which posits a new scale of economic organization transcending individual states. The global financial market is the classic case where private transactions in New York, London and Tokyo totally dominate the public currency reserves of any one country. If societies are built upon their economies then it would seem that crucial aspects of what we think of as societal relations should now be viewed beyond the state, perhaps even globally. This contemporary argument is a controversial one which is considered further in later chapters. Here I want to extend its implications historically. Although unusual in its scale and intensity, the current financial market is by no means unique in its geographical scale of operation. There were many important economic transactions beyond states which existed in previous centuries. Transcending states has been an integral part of economic development and in the argument of this book contemporary globalization is a culmination of these processes and not a new departure. From this long-term perspective, the modern world is viewed as a system of interconnected economic linkages. It is a 'world', not in the sense of global, but as the broad geographical area through which people and their social relations, loosely society, are able to be reproduced – that is, to have a history. Immanuel Wallerstein (1979) calls this the modern world-system which he dates from the expansion of Europe in the 'long' sixteenth century (1450–1650) and which eliminated all other social systems to become global in the twentieth century; hence today this social world does equate with global.

The corollary of this position is that since all members of this system are part of the same story-and-map, they are all deemed to be modern. Whatever their skills and attitudes, all people in the modern world-system have specifically modern roles within the larger whole. This is true of the three women introduced earlier despite their seemingly traditional roles as victims. The social glue which links their stories together is the way capital accumulation by others basically determines their lives. The modern world-system is a capitalist world-economy wherein the dominant social logic is ceaseless capital accumulation. This fundamental materialism within modern society is the great producer of modern victims. For instance, material linkages across the centuries between the three women may be as follows. The African woman snatched out of a non-modern world and forced into plantation labour produces sugar for the new coffee houses of England. In the process she contributes to the profits, not only of the plantation owner, but also of the Liverpool sugar merchant who delivers her wares to market. Striving for social respectability, this merchant manages to marry his daughter into the aristocratic land-owning classes, in this case a Protestant Irish family. As part of the Protestant ascendancy in Ireland it is a descendant of the sugar merchant who a century later has to make decisions on what to do with tenants unable to make payment on their land. As a progressive landowner versed with the latest political economy opinion, he realizes that eviction is both necessary and proper and this is how the young Irish woman finds herself on the road to Dublin. After much distress and trepidation she ends up in the relative security of the Irish community in Boston. Generations later and her descendants are happy to see

John F. Kennedy become the first Catholic President of the USA. A short time after the assassination, one descendant is called up for active service in Vietnam to do his patriotic duty against godless communism. It is during a short term of 'recreation' away from the fighting that this young man encounters the young Thai woman in a Bangkok brothel. They do not know each other of course, but they are linked together by much more than the commercial sex transacted that particular afternoon. One story, one map, all modern.

Whose modern?

Deeming all people within the modern world-system to be modern does not make them equal, of course. The three women above remain victims whatever we choose to call them. The modern world is a very differentiated world in both space and time. One of the problems of calling it modern is that it tends to suggest a homogeneous, or at least a homogenizing, world when all that the geohistorical interpretation argues is connectivity. Hence the question of power must be kept to the fore (Slater, 1996): whose modern world-system is it? Part of the difficulty arises from the word modern itself, which has temporal but not spatial referents. Modern society implies contemporary society plus the antecedents that created it which between them define the modern period. Without such a specific spatial connotation, once in this period, modern can be treated as a universal process. But, of course, the development of the modern world was anything but ageographical (King, 1995). Certain people and places are intimately implicated in its creation and growth and this is expressed in alternative 'geographical' descriptions of the process of modernization as Europeanization or Americanization or Westernization.

The modern world-system was originally created and developed through the spread of Europeans across the world as conquerors, settlers and traders. Like all migrants with the requisite power, they tried to recreate their new worlds in the image of their old so that the modern world grew in part as Europe writ large. By the twentieth century many non-European elites in Africa and Asia were Europeanized in the sense that they were educated in the schools and universities of the metropolitan centre or in new local educational establishments which purposively copied the latter. Thus by the time of worldwide decolonization after World War II, almost without exception the leaders of the new independent states were modernizing elites entering politics with European qualifications (Davidson, 1992). This meant that Europeanization did not end with decolonization but the new states, usually with constitutions modelled on that of their 'mother country', continued to have strong links with their erstwhile masters. The British Commonwealth and French Community are the political faces of this fact.

However, while this Europeanization was occurring in the 'South', in the 'North' a different transference was happening. The twentieth century has been an era of Americanization, a projection of US power through both coercion and consensus. One of the key periods of such projection was in Western Europe after World War II. Hence Europeanization of Africa went on simultaneously with the Americanization of Europe. In Europe this meant adopting and adapting US economic practices so that in the 1950s Western Europe began to experience the 'affluent society' pioneered by the USA (Duignan and Gann, 1992). Of course, American power was experienced in the South as a coercive force; this was where the North's 'Cold War' was allowed to grow hot in numerous wars, with the USA sometimes fighting them, other times using local surrogates (Chomsky and Herman, 1979). American social scientists may have preferred to use the universal term modernization at this time but the popular descriptions of Cocacolarization, Disnification, McWorld and the Levi generation leave no doubt as to its geographical provenance.

The idea of the world geographical division of North–South was devised in the 1970s as a means for diverting attention away from the Cold War and towards world poverty by placing the USA and USSR (plus Europe and Japan) in the same category. Although the Cold War was specified geographically as East versus West, this division is actually much older than the rise of either the USA or USSR. Thus East–West tensions have not ended with the demise of its particular manifestation as Cold War. Older civilization conflicts most notably relating to Islam have come to the fore as resistance to Westernization. In Muslim states the modernizing elites, such as

Kemal Ataturk's group in Turkey, attempted to Westernize their countries, for instance by adopting the Western alphabet, but with only partial success. There, and in Egypt and Algeria – all three countries have genuine modern revolutionary credentials – Westernization is being fiercely resisted by those who want to live in a non-Western Islamic society. In this case the term Westernization is particularly appropriate since it combines both the USA and Europe as a single threat but with the former as leader – Iran's 'Great Satan' no less.

These various geographical locatings of modernization are important but they do not necessarily lead us to a critical geohistorical understanding. Very often behind these ideas, and behind modernization itself, there is a taken-for-granted geohistorical perspective which combines a Whig history with a diffusionist geography. The former is defined as history whose story celebrates the present (Carr, 1961). This takes the form of defining important features of contemporary society and tracing their lineage back in time so that the story told is one which culminates in the success of today's society. Nineteenth-century English history is the classic case of this school of history in which the torch of progress was passed on, starting in ancient Mesopotamia, Egypt and Greece, until finding its final resting place in Victorian English hands. Diffusionist geography is the spatial equivalent of the latter. In this case the important features of contemporary society are traced geographically in order to show that all progress emanates from the centre of the modern world-system, first Europe and then the USA (Blaut, 1993). Mid-twentieth-century American development theory is the classic case here, with its assumption that modern American values could diffuse, even 'trickle down', to the rest of the world. Cutting out the ancient roots (except perhaps Europe's representative, classical 'democratic' Greece) from the history roster to focus on modern examples allows for the construction of a Whig-diffusionist geohistorical world view: England passing on the torch of liberty and progress to its American 'cousins' across the sea to spread around the world. The contemporary form of this Whig-diffusionalism appears as technological determinism with respect to advances in transport and communications. The resulting 'time–space compression' is at the heart of many views on globalization. In particular, David Harvey (1989) traces this 'speeding up of society' only to be criticized for both his partial history (Thrift, 1997) and his limited geography (Massey, 1993). The critics make the points that the 'crisis' of 'speeding up' is a common historical feature of modern society and that, in any case, for vast numbers of people in many places of the modern world such changes merely pass them by. How can we transcend the inherent partial history and limited geography of all Whig-diffusionalism?

The alternative to a Whig-diffusionist story-and-map, whether of the virtuous modern morality or deterministic modern technology variety, is to emphasize discontinuities in *both* time and space. Modernity does not just appear as a result of any 'natural' evolution; there are many discontinuities, with both the rise and the development of the modern world creating quite different forms of what it is to be modern. Similarly, the modern does not simply exist as a continuous geographical gradient from high to low: there are discontinuities between core and periphery zones of the system creating quite different forms of what it is to be modern. In short there are different modern times and different modern spaces in a world of multiple modernities.

1

Modern, -ity, -ism, -ization

The concepts and images which have been derived from the simple notion of modern constitute an amazing cluster of related ideas. As well as its promiscuity as an adjective, historically modern can be a noun, usually in the plural as in the famous late seventeenth-century intellectual debate between the 'moderns' and the 'ancients'. Today, the social scientist's favoured concept is modernity. According to David Lyon (1994, p. 27), this concept 'is a phenomenon of great diversity and richness, hard, if not impossible, to summarise'. But that has certainly not stopped people trying because, it seems, modernity is 'both so irresistible and so problematic a category' (Osborne, 1996, p. 348). I agree with both of these sentiments and will immediately complicate matters further by extending consideration to two further concepts derived from being modern: modernism with its modernists and modernization with its modernizers.

Modernity, modernism and modernization have very different provenances: each concept was developed in quite different contexts for quite different purposes. Their changing saliences for social science are illustrated by their historical appearances in standard works of reference. Taking three examples at approximately thirty-year intervals the following sequence appears: in the 1933 edition of *Encyclopaedia of Social Sciences* there is only an entry for 'modernism', defined as an 'attitude of mind' in the art world (Kallen,

1933, p. 564); in the 1968 edition of *International Encyclopedia of Social Sciences* there is only an entry for 'modernization', defined as social change for developing countries, their 'pictures of the future' (Lerner, Coleman and Dore, 1968, pp. 386–7); and in the 1996 edition of *The Social Science Encyclopedia* there is an entry for 'modernity', defined as cultural, social and economic change which is 'inherently globalizing' (Archetti, 1996, p. 546). Despite this immensely wide range of applications – from an art movement to economic development planning to globalization – I will treat these three concepts as constituting a single cluster of ideas: they have a common concern for newness and change, sometimes celebrating change, other times trying to control it.

Of the three concepts, modernism is distinct in developing outside social science but is no less interesting for that. The modernist movement and the new discipline of sociology provided alternative critical views of the modern world at the turn of the nineteenth century. The artistic creations of modernism were unsettling because the movement attacked realism and suggested that all was not as it appeared in the modern world. Go into any modern art gallery today and you can still feel the challenge to come to terms with images which force new ways of thinking. Similarly, sociologists argued all was not as it seemed with 'modern society'; they discovered a dark side to being modern. The founding fathers of social theory, each in their distinct way, unveiled this downside: 'alienation', 'anomie', 'iron cage' and 'anonymity' discovered at the heart of modern society by Marx, Durkheim, Weber and Simmel respectively (Lyon, 1994, p. 28). Although very different in detail, each theorist produced a sort of Jekyll and Hyde theory of being modern, recognizing the advantages of 'progress' while identifying the price that had to be paid for it. Basically these theorists challenged the supposed link between modernity and liberty, arguing that for ordinary people the onset of modernity was associated with loss of freedom and autonomy. However, by the mid-twentieth century the idea of modernization, as the process leading to modern society, became caught up in Cold War rivalries in relation to third world countries. In this context, a 'Dr Jekyll only' social theory was created, modern society shorn of its downside. Devising development models to counter the attractions of communism to poor third world countries, first world societies were treated unambiguously as success stories to be emulated. Hence, the resulting 'modernization theory' was fully committed to poor countries becoming modern, with the negative ideas of alienation, anomie, iron cage and anonymity conveniently ignored or neglected. In a sense, therefore, social scientists in the 1950s and 1960s performed the role of advertising agents for the West in the battle for the third world. But, whether the suffixes to modern are -ity, -ism or -ization, this cannot hide the common experience upon which they are based. I will employ modernity as an umbrella term, the cluster name if you will, to cover all these experiences (with their various suffixes); it is the condition of living in a modern society. And the emphasis here is on society; the meaning of modernity is not just societal in scope: it denotes a defining nature of a society.

Ambiguous to the core

The credibility of modernization theory as applied to third world countries declined rapidly in the 1970s. In contemporary social theory the word most associated with modernity is ambiguity. From the modernizers' interest in building stable social structures, attention has turned to the idea of modern as the fleeting, and the consequent disorientation which comes with incessant social change. Concern for this 'other' modern was stimulated largely by the publication of Marshall Berman's (1988) *All that is Solid Melts into Air*, first published in 1982. The result has been that social scientists have had to come to terms with two 'faces' of the modern (Lash and Friedman, 1992, p. 2): 'order and chaos are *modern* twins' (Bauman, 1991, p. 4; emphasis in the original). And, of course, the really intriguing thing about this double meaning of modernity is that the two are polar opposites. Recently this has been well captured both by Peter Wagner (1994) in his treatment of modernity as an interplay between liberty on the one hand and discipline on the other, and by Boaventura de Sousa Santos (1995, p. 2) in his discussion of the 'two pillars' of modernity, regulation and emancipation. Hence modernity is one of those rare concepts with a contradiction inherent in its meaning.

According to Marshall Berman (1988, p. 15), to live in the modern world is to live in 'a maelstrom of perpetual disintegration and renewal, of struggle and contradiction, of ambiguity and anguish'. The modernism movement which burst on to the arts scene a century ago explicitly provided the visions and images to try to capture, or make sense of, the maelstrom of modern life. Of course, coping with modernity extends far beyond artistic movements; ordinary people have to deal with it in their daily lives. To live in the modern world is a very paradoxical affair. Men and women experience rapid change both as opportunity for a better world and as destroyer of their existing world. In this context modern behaviour can be viewed as the attempt to avoid being an object of change by becoming your own subject. Thus Berman (1992, p. 55) interprets 1989 as 'a great *modernist* year' because the peoples of Eastern Europe were 'all trying to make the modern world their own'. But more generally, since you cannot stop the world and get off, avoiding being an object will mean attempting a partial shielding from a threatening world of uncertainty and change. For instance, for the ordinary working man in late nineteenth-century American cities, saloons and liquor provided one haven from an unpalatable world, while the Temperance Movement promoted an alternative haven, home and family. Both represented ways to 'tame the modern', albeit only temporarily.

Containerization is a generic means for taming the modern. Whether retreating into a favoured tavern or his own dwelling, the working man above was entering a bounded place to find comfort through leaving an insecure world outside. At a larger scale, the modern state is premised upon territoriality, both people and commodities are controlled at the border to provide opportunity to control content of a given sovereign territory. This is an opportunity political regimes which portray themselves as agents of modernity have taken advantage of. Emphasizing rationality as a core property of modernity, they have attempted to control change through bureaucratic planning. Political elites in revolutionary and Napoleonic France were explicit modernizers as they rationalized the government of their own country and then attempted to export their modern bureaucracy to the rest of Europe – Woolf (1991, p. 13) refers to this as 'the administrative project for modernity'. In more recent times the USSR thought it could capture modernity in its planning mechanism and so steer change in its preferred direction. Both of these projects were spectacular failures, their bureaucracies proving to be far too crude a mechanism for successful social engineering and unable to cope with the modern maelstrom – these, and other similar projects, can slide quite rapidly from the 'renewal' to the 'disintegration' side of modernity. However, although modernity cannot be captured by a particular state apparatus, that does not mean that particular states are never implicated in the renewal aspect of the modern, as I will argue in the next chapter. By taking advantage of opportunities that arise, states can certainly nurture modernity for their own ends; in certain circumstances they may generate new forms of modernity.

Planning is not, of course, the sole property of revolutionary states. In fact all organizations have to plan for the future in order to have a future. Corporations, large and small, define strategic plans as part of the ordinary business of doing business. Without the limits of territoriality, modern corporations try to assess current trends and future possibilities as they position themselves to take advantage of predicted change. At the turn of the nineteenth century, at approximately the same time modernists were attempting to capture change on their canvases, there were numerous 'planning movements' geared to controlling change in several practical fields. For instance, 'urban planning' was created to impose order on the chaotic nineteenth-century city, and the new 'management science' was devised to plan maximum efficiency in business. I shall call these attempts to plan and manage the future, and thus to tame change, modernity projects. Despite their great variety, such projects share one basic property: to define an order within the modern maelstrom.

One way in which the ambiguity of modernity operates can now be understood. Modern people and institutions devise projects which aspire to order their world but without fully appreciating that the modern world is the antithesis of order. Modernity, therefore, is a perpetual battle between makers of order and the incessant change which is the condition of modernity. Obviously institutions and individuals vary widely in the successes of their projects and, in particular, in terms of how long their projects remain viable. In a perpetually changing world, all projects inevitably become out of date as soon as they begin to operate. They may be maintained by adapting to new circumstances but in the modern maelstrom they all eventually succumb to disintegration and are replaced by new projects. In recent years Soviet economic planning, third world development planning, welfare state social planning, Cold War military planning, urban land use planning and Fordist corporate planning have all faced disintegration and have disappeared or been reformed to be replaced by new models incorporating rather less order.

Confusion over modernity's ambiguity arises when the modernizers do not realize the sheer size of their task. Believing the future to be on its side, the USSR confidently planned its path in five-year steps to overtake the USA before the end of the twentieth century. Once again, however, you do not need to be a revolutionary to fall into this trap: the American diplomat Paul Hoffman (1962, p. 142) predicted that 'By the year 2000, we can all be living in a world that has overcome poverty.' Thus was modernization theory, that most American social science model, similarly imbued with a false optimism. Third world countries under Western tutelage embarked upon development plans to banish 'under-development' through stable and orderly economic growth. Subsequent criticism of these projects has concentrated on the fact that the economic growth record of these poorer countries has been variable and disappointing, although what has subsequently happened to the richer countries is equally relevant.

Since the 1960s many third world economies have stagnated at best, making their popular designation as 'developing countries' ring rather hollow. In contrast the 'developed countries', as richer countries are euphemistically termed, have been the locus of most important changes in economic practices since the early 1980s. This despite the fact that the adjective 'developed' implies an end-state, the final condition of development. Hence the very modern irony that it has been the rich countries which are, by and large, the 'developing states'. This should be no surprise taking a long-term view: in times of worldwide economic downturn it is the rich and powerful who are best equipped to preserve and expand what they have. But in the optimistic post-World War II boom, few voices thought the widespread and historically high levels of economic growth could not be continually sustained. Put simply, modernization theorists, like Soviet planners, had a one-sided, simplistic understanding of modernity.

Social theory with smoke in its eyes

Popular ideas on being modern, modernist artists, sociology's founding fathers, American modernization theorists and Soviet planners
have all shared one common image of modernity. In both common
language and theoretical discourses, modern and industrial have
gone together like inseparable twins: the phrases 'industrial society' and 'modern society' have been seen as synonyms. This way of
thinking can be traced back to the impact of industrialization on
the idea of progress (Kumar, 1978, p. 48): the eighteenth-century
Enlightenment's concern for social progress had been framed in
abstract terms, the subsequent social upheavals that resulted from
the industrial revolution gave progress its concrete content. It
remains quite remarkable the way that modern and industrial
have been interchangeable adjectives for describing twentieth-
century society and its world. Despite the fact that the constel-
lation of ideas that constitute the former – progress, rationality,
freedom, science – clearly predate the industrial revolution, the
latter's image and reality have been so powerful as to totally dominate social thinking, both practical and theoretical. Participants in
the modernism movement, for example, were fascinated by machines as the instigators of change.

It is in social theory where the idea of modern as industrial has
been most developed. Such theory was very much an interpretation
derived from nineteenth-century experience: it was the world of
rapid industrial growth and associated mass urbanization that the
social theorists were trying to understand and come to terms with.
Thus, despite important differences between the various theorists,
one similarity stood out: the various theories were all built upon an
opposition between industrial/modern and agricultural/traditional.
This dualism has permeated social theory through most of the
twentieth century. Thus mid-century modernization theory was
premised upon the practice of industrialization: modernization was
dependent upon economic development which was interpreted as
industrialization. The latter was seen as the 'panacea' for all third
world countries: 'Modern civilization is based upon iron and steel
and the establishment of iron and steel works is one of the most
desired features of planned development' (Mountjoy, 1963, p. 146).

Eastern European communist states also embarked on this road to industrialization; the prospect was the same in both cases, namely the very same 'industrial society' which was the subject matter of standard social theory.

This modern/industrial equation has had one crucial debilitating effect: modernity has been presented as a singular condition of society. I will call this the industrial presumption: there is only one modernity and it is industrial. But this presumption has not gone unchallenged; while it incorporates the idea that 'pre-industrial' societies are not modern, what of 'post-industrial' societies? With the 1970s rise of the idea that Western societies were becoming 'post-industrial', the ongoing logic of this situation was to declare, therefore, that society had become 'post-modern'. There is, however, a second position which I favour: the concept of post-industrial provides the opportunity to liberate modern from a singular industrial condition. The time has finally arrived when social theory is rubbing the smoke from its eyes and breaking the yoke of industry on the idea of being modern. With this liberation, the taboo on thinking of more than one modernity is thus broken.

Multiple moderns versus multiple modernities

Having escaped from social theory's fixation on the nineteenth century, it soon becomes clear that other intellectual approaches to understanding the modern have very different ideas about its origin. The eighteenth-century Enlightenment is a particularly popular source for modernity, but it is also commonplace to go back even further: for instance, Santos (1995) focuses upon scientific rationality and traces modernity to the seventeenth century while Toulmin's (1990) concern for critical humanism pushes his modernity back to the sixteenth-century Renaissance. In the other direction, the modernism movement was proclaiming its new modern age in the realm of aesthetics at the last *fin de siècle* just when classical social theory was equating the birth of the modern with the century that was disappearing. This immense confusion in timing on something as basic as the origin of the modern world is in keeping with modernity's ambiguity and, indeed, it brings the first two sections of this chapter together: modern social theory has failed to 'intellectually tame' modernity by classifying it as solely industrial. The question now is, how to proceed beyond the singular interpretation of modernity bequeathed by social theory.

Any credible approach to this question has to accommodate the consequent plurality of being modern. There have been two distinct ways of answering this question which I simplify as 'multiple moderns' and 'multiple modernities'. The first defines a sectional plurality and is decisively analytic in temper. That is to say, the idea of being modern is broken down into its component parts. It is thus divisive, treating, for instance, modern economics and modern politics as separate and autonomous processes. I take the second approach, which privileges synthesis over analysis. This treats being modern as a coherent combination of social processes, using such all-encompassing ideas as modern worlds and modern times. Thus, in the next chapter, I will deal with three consecutive modern worlds and times: a mercantile modernity created largely by the seventeenth-century Dutch, an industrial modernity created largely by the eighteenth- and nineteenth-century British, and a consumer modernity created largely by twentieth-century Americans. The contrast between the analysis of moderns and the synthesis of modernities is a stark one.

The remainder of this section consists of a critique of the multiple moderns approach partly as a means of justifying my own geohistory. In addition, the critique is important because it provides an opportunity of showing how a geohistorical approach can transcend some theoretical problems which seem intractable within social theory. In short, I will argue that if a theoretical problem is the result of abstracting social relations from their context, then it can be avoided in a geohistorical approach. That is to say, instead of the problem being intrinsic, it is merely an unintended consequence of a particular methodology. For readers with less concern for social theory who want to proceed to see how I begin to treat the three modernities I have just identified, you may wish to skip the following argument and move on directly to the next section on the 'modernization of modernities'.

Treating different sectors of social relations separately is the norm in social science; in fact it defines the core disciplines of economics, sociology and political science. Focusing attention on different groups of separate processes is one important way in which social scientists have distinguished their work from Marxist historical materialism. To the extent that the latter was interpreted as a deterministic theory with the 'economic base' ultimately explaining all, most social scientists opted for a more flexible approach where the different aspects of social life could be allotted separate determinations. This approach worked well in many research contexts but its limitations are revealed when it is confronted by the simple, holistic notion of a modern world, of modernity as a general social condition covering all aspects of social life. Multiple moderns remains, nevertheless, a very common approach. Here I will focus my critique largely upon an Open University sociology textbook (Hall, 1992) which exemplifies the multiple moderns approach.

Stuart Hall (1992, p. 1) begins where I begin, by breaking from what he calls the 'tradition' of identifying modern societies 'with the onset of industrialization in the nineteenth century'. But then he goes on to refuse to provide a 'precise date when modern societies began' (p. 8). This is not another ahistorical argument; his reluctance to be pinned down historically is because he interprets modernity as a result of 'different processes, working according to different time-scales' (p. 1). Four 'major social processes' are identified – political, economic, social and cultural – and the transition to modernity consists of their interactions (p. 5). The result is 'a more plural conception of the historical process' which emphasises diversity and difference over similarity and uniformity (p. 11). He is particularly keen to promote a multi-causal rather than mono-causal explanation of modernity. This is the heart of the matter: the requirement to avoid, at all costs, suspicion of the economic reductionism which underlies important variants of both Marxist theory and modernization theory. Hall (1992, p. 10) admits 'the link between capitalism and modernity' but argues that the diversity in outcomes of modern societies – France, for example, is different from Japan – proves that the economic is not determining, the other three social processes being just as important.

The relationship between capitalism and modernity has also been of particular concern for Santos (1995) and Wood (1997) in their recent writings and they both come to similar conclusions to Hall. The first sentence of Santos's book reads (p. 1): 'Modernity and capitalism are two different and autonomous historical processes.' Wood is even blunter, asserting that to identify modernity with capitalism 'is a fundamental mistake' (p. 539). Both sustain their arguments empirically in terms of the physical separation of the two processes. Wood equates modernity with the Enlightenment project which 'belongs to a distinctively non-capitalist society', pre-revolutionary France. The latter is contrasted to England as the birthplace of capitalism. Santos has modernity emerging in the six-teenth century well before capitalism became dominant in the nine-teenth century. But what happens when the physical separation ends? For Santos (p. 1), after 1800 'the two historical processes converged and interpenetrated each other, but in spite of that, the conditions and dynamics of their development remained separate and relatively autonomous'. Hence Santos brings up the old theor-etical conundrum of relative autonomy, the neo-Marxist formula for avoiding reductionism. How relative? Relative to what? How can processes that interpenetrate one another be autonomous in any realistic sense? Hall (1992) does not describe his 'different processes' as autonomous because 'they were articulated with one another' but 'they weren't inevitably harnessed together' (p. 9). The use of the term 'inevitably' shows his sensitivity for avoiding deter-minism yet it would seem Hall confuses what could have happened with what did happen. Previously (p. 5) he had reminded us that despite the 'different histories' of his four processes, 'in "real" historical time, they interacted with one another'. And that is really the point, the fact cannot be avoided that for some, albeit con-tested, of the period over the last half-millennium, modern states, modern economies, modern societies and modern cultures all existed together reinforcing one another in so many ways that we call the outcome the modern world.

One of Hall's (1992, p. 7) reasons for studying modernity in terms of four different processes is that they mirror a 'particular feature' of modern societies, their articulation into 'distinct, clearly demarcated zones of activity'. But by organizing explanation of modernity into different histories of these 'domains' or 'spheres' – 'the polity, the economy, the social structure and the cultural sphere' – there must be the danger, at best of undervaluing the connect-ions, and at worst of missing the overall nature of what it is to be modern. This division into spheres of activity is certainly 'partic-ular' to modernity, but such a singularity implies a real possibility that the division is part of the essence of modernity, a necessary condition for its production and reproduction. Hence, by framing their explanations in this way, following modernity's own divisions, Hall and his colleagues may be dangerously weakening their capacity to understand their subject critically.

It is interesting that both Hall and Santos have trouble sustaining their divisive positions within their own texts. For instance, Santos (1995, p. 1) refers to capitalism as 'a part of modernity', which is certainly not consistent with his autonomy position. Similarly, Hall (1992, p. 9), after agreeing with the 'implausibility' of history 'unfolding according to one logic', finishes his discussion with reference to 'the logic of modernity' whose 'twists and turns' make up 'the modern story' (p. 16). This is all very reminiscent of the earlier world-systems debate on 'one logic or two' referring, in this case, to whether the economic and political were autonomous of one another in the international field (Chase-Dunn, 1981). In his argument for a single logic, Christopher Chase-Dunn (1981, p. 25) concludes that 'the logic of the accumulation process *includes* the logic of state building and geopolitics' (emphasis in original). This may sound a little too economic-determinist for current sensitivities but I still think the argument remains a strong one. Today I would describe this as the economic being embedded in the political and vice versa, where embeddedness implies the necessary context for a particular sphere of activities to be reproduced.

This is why Wallerstein (1979) has always referred to the modern world-system interchangeably as the capitalist world-economy. They are, as he puts it, two sides of the same coin: capitalism is embedded in modernity, modernity is embedded in capitalism. His position is strongly supported by the remarkable geohistorical congruence in treatments of capitalism and modernity as separate phenomena. For instance, like modernity, capitalism has its own industrial presumption: most social scientists have treated capitalist society as synonymous with industrial society. But the similarity extends further. Like modernity, locating the beginning of capitalism with industrialization is widely contested. And the second most popular choice of beginning, that of most historians and geographers, is also the same for both capitalism and modernity: the expansion of Europe in the sixteenth and early seventeenth centuries. In short, the geohistorical debates over capitalism have an uncanny resemblance to those concerning modernity. Viewing both modernity and capitalism as societal in scope, penetrating throughout society, amounts to two ways of looking at the same object, the contemporary world and its critical antecedents.

To return to Hall's (1992) four moderns, in the geohistorical approach pursued here, modern political relations, modern economic relations, modern societal relations and modern cultural relations are each embedded in the processes of the others. Each needs the other three for its own reproduction, hence all are equally necessary. They interact with one another differently in different times and places, notably between the three modernities identified earlier, but they remain all part of a modern world. Hence there is no need for concepts such as the relative autonomy of one process from another. Marxists devised this formulation, as a way of recognizing different processes while tracing the motor of change back to economics – capitalism – 'in the last instance' in Engels's famous phrase. Of course, in a geohistorical approach, the very notion of 'last instance' has no meaning; it is a metaphysics which has no relevance for geohistorical change.

Modernizations of modernities

Using the multiple modernities approach requires a rather odd new concept, the modernization of modernity. How can something that is modern be modernized? This question constitutes a problem only for those who insist on adhering to a static view of modernity. If, however, modernity represents incessant change, it follows that what was modern must become unmodern. This idea is commonplace as, for example, when heavy engineering complexes are described as 'traditional industry'. Such complexes were the cutting edge of modernity in the nineteenth century; in the latter decades of the twentieth-century the adjective, traditional, previously applied to the industry's nemesis, agriculture, is now used to describe this great industry with no thought of irony. Rather than being odd, therefore, modernization of modernity is a normal process. For instance, a recent article caught my eye by asking 'why France rejects modernity?' (Walden, 1997). Can this be the France of the Enlightenment, of the great revolution, of the great empire, of two world war victories, of the post-war industrial miracle? Of course, yes, the article is concerned for France bucking contemporary neo-liberal globalization trends, the current form of modernity.

The phrase modernization of modernity was coined by Ulrich Beck (1994) as part of his argument that industrial modernity is being transformed into a new reflexive modernity in what he terms contemporary risk society. Here I am not concerned with his theory as a whole but just his mechanism of transition from one modernity to another, a topic, for reasons given previously, rarely theorized. According to Scott Lash (1994, p. 112), the new theory of reflexive modernization represents 'a creative departure from the seemingly endless debates between modernists and postmodernists'. I agree with this assessment and am particularly drawn to their analysis because the theory admits that, contrary to the industrial presumption, 'many modernities are possible' (Beck, 1994, p. 24).

Beck breaks with the conventional idea that all fundamental social change results from social collapse, economic crisis and/or political revolution. He quotes Montesquieu approvingly: 'Institutions founder on their own success' (Beck, 1994, p. 1). Hence he develops a theory, not of crisis, but of success; the contemporary shift in modernity which he postulates is generated by the victory of modernization (p. 2). Transition from one modernity to another is created by the 'normal' workings of the existing modernity whose ultimate fulfilment is a new society. The terms Beck uses to describe this fundamental change provide the essence of the process being posited: 'surreptitious', 'unplanned', 'unintended', 'unpolitical' (p. 3). He argues that large cumulative effects can result from small measures with little or no political conflict. He gives the example of increasing participation of women in the workforce which 'leads to an upheaval snail's pace of the conventional occupational, political and private order of things' (p. 3). Such change is not the result of great debates in parliament or revolutionary actions; rather, it becomes widely accepted as a familiar and desirable feature of contemporary society which, nevertheless, conceals a 'society-changing scope' (p. 4). The formula is deceptively simple: 'The desired + the familiar = new modernity' (p. 4).

One way of interpreting Beck's model is that he takes seriously the 'other modernity' of flux and change, traditionally neglected by sociologists, so that all modernities have obsolescence programmed into their being: there are always 'new social contracts waiting to be born' (p. 1). The optimism generated by the initial success of a new form of modernity will give way eventually to 'a return of uncertainty' (p. 8) which Beck envisages operating through two phases (p. 5). First, the uncertainty is contained within existing social and political norms and is considered merely residual to the current orthodoxies. Here the 'self-concept' of the existing modernity prevails although the processes are in hand to overturn it. Second, a new situation arises when the uncertainty 'begins to dominate public, political and private debates and conflict' (p. 5). The old modernity becomes problematic but society hangs on to old institutions while new debates rage. This is to enter 'a double world' of a simultaneous disembedding and re-embedding of contrary social relations. There is a sense of society belonging to 'two different epochs' (pp. 16–17) with all the social chaos that that implies.

It follows that shifts in modernity can coincide with conventional sources of social change – crises and revolutions – and indeed may intensify them (Beck, 1994, p. 4). One obvious research direction is to explore the relations between them: crises as a 'success too far'? But it remains important to interpret modernizations of modernity and social crises as different processes. To the degree that 'crises' are identified within conventional politics they will be interpreted through the categories of the old modernity. But policies thus formed are more than likely to exacerbate the situation. The new modernity has evolved a very different agenda, a 'sub-politics' with distinctive 'sub-policies' (pp. 22–3) which Beck describes as 'a non-institutional renaissance of the political' (p. 17).

This sophisticated model of fundamental social change has been developed as a means of describing the contemporary transition to what Beck (1992) identifies as a new 'risk society'. Although I do not use his delineation of contemporary modernity, his model of modernization of modernity is central to my concerns.

2

Prime Modernities

In 1697, eight years after overthrowing his sister's regency, Tsar Peter the Great could be found working incognito as an apprentice in a Dutch shipyard. At first glance a bizarre happening, a little further thought marks it out as a typical story in the history of modernity. Peter is styled 'Great' because of his military prowess but he had enough nous to understand that in order to be successful in this traditional role he had to 'change with the times'. Peter was the great modernizer of Russia. His new capital of St Petersburg was created to be both a naval base and a trading centre and represents, according to Marshall Berman (1988, chapter IV), the first example of a non-Western country wrestling with the transition to modernity. This modernization of underdevelopment is about emulating the 'advanced' societies of the West in order to 'catch up'. Peter was working in the shipyard in order to understand the secrets of the technology that brings progress.

I will argue that this episode is symbolic of the perennial 'clash' between the modern and the traditional that marks the modern historical era. I have problematized the word clash with inverted commas because of an ambiguity resulting from the mutuality in relations between the two sides of the duality: tsars, even Peter, were arch-typically traditional in their ultimate pursuits but periodically found the need to modernize. Their tradition existed in a modern world which could not be ignored. If this interpretation of Peter the great modernizer as a symbol of modern–traditional relations is accepted, several interesting corollaries follow. First, the technology being learned does not fit our image of 'industrial': wood and wind defined the production process, not mechanical engineering based upon iron and coal. Second, the shipyard is located in the Netherlands not France or England which, from the eighteenth century, have vied for the title of birthplace of modernity. Third, and related to the other two, this episode precedes the Enlightenment, the French Revolution and the industrial revolution, each of which has been claimed as creator of the modern world. In short, Peter the Great points in a different direction, to the seventeenth-century Dutch as the people to emulate, that is to say, the Dutch as creators of a most modern society. I follow Peter's lead in this chapter.

World hegemony as uneven social change

The concepts of modernity and hegemony come from two rather different theoretical traditions and have not been, therefore, usually considered within the same analysis. But they are not so far apart as may at first appear. If the watchword of modernity is change, the equivalent for hegemony is stability. Thus the stability of hegemonic social relations can be interpreted as a taming of social change. In this simple logic, a hegemonic agent is a producer of a particular modernity. Rapid change may be the norm in the modern world-system, but there is no reason to assume the rate of social change to be coped with is constant. There are many social theories which emphasize the unevenness of change both over space, as core–periphery at different scales, and over time, as cycles of varying lengths. I will argue that world hegemony defines a particularly acute uneven pattern of social change in both time and space. To develop such an approach, however, requires a revision in the scale of societal relations as traditionally conceived in studies of hegemony.

The most sophisticated treatments of hegemony in social analyses have been stimulated by the Italian Marxist Antonio Gramsci (Hoare and Smith, 1971). He explained the relatively high level of consensus in the stable liberal democracies of the period between World

Wars I and II by the particular dominance of their bourgeoisies. These were deemed hegemonic situations because the ideas of the ruling class were the ruling ideas of society. The corollary was that there was less need to use the coercive arm of the state to keep subordinate classes in order, hence the relatively stable politics in the liberal democracies. In this formulation the political subjects – the 'actors' – are social classes and the political object is the state and its society. In the analysis employed here, the concept of hegemony is used at a different scale of operation: the subjects are the states with their civil societies and the object is the modern world-system. Hence I use the term world hegemony on account of the object through which the consensual processes are deemed to operate.

Hegemonic states are particular core states that appear at specific conjunctures in the development of the modern world-system and are implicated crucially in the overall development of the system. Three hegemonic cycles representing the rise, achievement and demise of hegemonic status by the Netherlands, Britain and the USA over the last four centuries have been identified. They represent the longest 'waves' in the unfolding of the history of the modern world-system (Wallerstein, 1984). At the peak of each cycle, referred to as 'high hegemony', the hegemonic states have not just been great powers, or even *primus inter pares*, they had 'something extra' that marked them out as qualitatively different from their rivals (Arrighi, 1990; 1994). World hegemons were initially defined by their pre-eminent success in capital accumulation. Wallerstein (1984) emphasizes their initial productive economic edge which feeds into commercial advantage and culminates in them becoming the financial centre of the world-economy. Hence the latter has moved from Amsterdam to London to New York over the last four hundred years. High hegemony as the apogee of the cycle is defined economically when the production, commercial and financial successes occur together. Given such a dominance of the world market, the state in question becomes a liberal champion of the world-economy: the Dutch promote *mare liberum*, the British free trade and the Americans free enterprise. In each case the special interests of the hegemon have been presented as universal interests for the whole system in classic Gramscian mode (Taylor, 1996a). Thus although previous world-systems studies have focused upon the political economy characteristics of world hegemony, there is no analytical reason why

Gramsci's more 'cultural hegemony' should not also operate at this world level. World hegemons have provided, to use Gramsci's terminology, 'moral and intellectual leadership' within the inter-state system which has had a fundamental impact upon the socio-cultural nature of the modern world-system.

Although not primarily defined in terms of military prowess, high hegemony has nevertheless been ushered in by world war victories. The rise phase of each hegemony cycle has been marked by a period of what Arrighi (1990) calls systemic chaos, when the hegemon becomes both financier and productive arsenal of the eventual winning coalition. The end result of these wars – the Thirty Years War (1618–48), the Revolutionary and Napoleonic Wars (1792–1815) and World Wars I and II (1914–45) – has been to provide the hegemon with a unique opportunity for world leadership. In each case, while all main rivals, both allies and enemies, have been devastated by war, the hegemon had a 'good war' in the sense that its economy was greatly boosted by the war. Hence the hegemonic state emerges from world war immensely superior to all other states; it is the great exception in a time of chaos, able to show others what form post-war reconstruction should take. High hegemony is achieved politically when those wielding power within the hegemon use this opportunity to create a new world in their own image.

It is important to note that hegemonic cycles do not simply repeat themselves; rather, they constitute a spiral of change. This is expressed in Arrighi's (1990) treatment of world hegemony as stages of world development: he identifies three different forms of international politics and capitalism each associated with major hegemonic restructurings of the inter-state system and the capitalist world-economy respectively. Returning to the concept of modern world-system, and translating this spiral to becoming and being modern, suggests the production of three prime modernities, one Dutch, one British and one American. Here I shall interpret each world hegemon as the most modern of the modern of its respective era of supremacy.

Three prime modernities

The three modernities I deal with here are Dutch-led mercantile modernity, British-led industrial modernity and American-led consumer modernity. Of all the many modernities which may be identified, I call these three prime because of their direct association with world hegemony. Their hegemonic nature means that they penetrate societal relations throughout the system within their era. In fact, they invade and pervade so much that they transcend their hegemonic state origins to provide the common labels for their respective times: the age of mercantilism, the industrial age and the consumer age respectively. Quite simply, they define three modern worlds.

The idea of their being three prime modernities is broadly consistent with other overviews of modernity which trace being modern to before the industrial revolution. Berman (1988, pp. 16–17), for instance, identifies three main phases of modernity, the first extending from the sixteenth to the eighteenth centuries, the second in the nineteenth century and a contemporary modernity in the twentieth century. At the cultural-ideological level these phases can be defined as intellectual attempts to order knowledge so that people are subjects as well as objects of social change. Three periods of major ordering are usually identified: in the seventeenth century a Cartesian world was devised with 'man' at the centre, the nineteenth century was the high mark of change interpreted as human progress and in the twentieth century the idea of change has been repackaged as development in modernization theory. Each of these is a theoretical taming of the perpetually new by application of a rationality privileging science and technology. Adding hegemony to the argument locates a critical source of this disturbing and stimulating newness. Since the rate of change will accelerate precisely when hegemons are creating a new political economy through their restructuring of the world-economy, it is to be expected that this will stimulate a basic need for intellectual reassessments: a rationalization of the newness is required. Hence Berman's three phases of modernity can be interpreted as the cultural-ideological reaction to hegemonic creation of social uncertainties.

Underpinning this 'high' modernity of the intellectuals there is the modernity lived by ordinary people. Each hegemon has been responsible for creating its particular version of what is modern about the modern world-system. Unlike the overt state modernizers who have attempted to tame modernity through planning,

hegemonic states and their civil societies have been covert modernizers. They have operated within a particularly successful trajectory of social change, reinforcing it by their activities and without
the need to try to control change. Thus instead of simple planning,
a more complex mix of political and economic elite behaviour is
rewarded in the world market creating the success story which is
hegemony. For a short period it even seems that the world-economy
is working for the hegemon and the modern world-system is the
hegemon writ large as, for instance, when the twentieth century is
called the 'American Century'.

Mercantile modernity was created through the everyday life of
commerce and the massive coterie of activities that it generated.
There had, of course, been many influential networks of merchants
in the past but in the seventeenth century a new rationality came
to dominate success in the world-system in which the calculating
behaviour of the merchant was the archetypal practical form. The
Dutch, more than anyone else, made making money respectable.
Navigation became the great enabling applied science and new
market institutions (e.g. the Bourse) were invented as Amsterdam
became the first modern information centre in the world (W. D.
Smith, 1984). It is in the second half of the seventeenth century
that the idea of a self-consciously modern world appears. These
were attempts to make sense of the changes occurring which seemed
to make Western Europe appear to be more 'advanced' than
Europe's erstwhile golden age, classical Greece and Rome. The intellectual victory of the 'moderns' over the 'ancients' culminated in
the eighteenth-century Enlightenment with its abstract theories of
progress and where the seventeenth-century Dutch were viewed, in
Voltaire's words, as a 'terrestrial paradise' (Schama, 1981, p. 56).

In the late eighteenth and nineteenth centuries industrial modernity was created through a new scale of production: new energy
(steam engine), new machines, new factories. This made new levels
of capital accumulation possible in concentrated zones of production: great commercial ports gave way to massive industrial
towns and regions as the archetypal modern. There is no doubt
that Britain is the country most implicated in bringing this second
modern condition about. In this industrial world, modern society
became mass society – the modern became, in Marx's terms, an
alienated way of life for people leaving the land to sell their labour

in mine and factory. Mechanical engineering became the enabling knowledge as new machines of iron and steel became the cutting edge of change. The 'Victorian cult of progress' was based upon the successes of technology and created an inordinate faith in the future. This is how, with industrialization, the British gave the Enlightenment idea of progress a concrete manifestation, making it the dominant organizing principle for understanding social change, both popular and intellectual.

In the twentieth century the social effects of alienation have been countered in selected countries by a spread of affluence to ordinary people. According to Kenneth Galbraith (1958, p. 13) this circumstance was historically unprecedented. The USA has been the major creator of this new consumer modernity as suburbia and its ubiquitous shopping mall have become the focal modern place. This modernity is defined by a uniquely close relation between mass production and mass consumption. New production practices based upon 'scientific management' (Taylorism) and the birth of modern advertising in the decades before World War I set the basis for this new modernity. As more and more is produced, the focus moves clearly on to consumption in order to realize the capital. It is at this time that progress is repackaged as development but loses none of its social optimism, promising 'high mass consumption' for all as modernization. Management science becomes the new enabling knowledge culminating in the merging of computers and communication in the late twentieth century.

One final point needs to be emphasized about these modernities. They represent three distinct episodes within a single system, not three new systems. In terms of their political economies, for instance, at all times commodities had to be made (production), distributed (commerce) and sold (consumption); what each hegemon achieved was a particular structuring of these relations in which one of these three activities was particularly emphasized. As far as socio-cultural relations are concerned, there is much overlap between the respective eras – the subject matter of the next chapter – but there is no ignoring the distinct political economy, *mentalité* and way of life which dominated three modern worlds in practice and in aspiration. This is best illustrated by focusing on the transitions or shifts between the modernities I have identified.

Two modernizations of modernities

Shifts between the prime modernities can be described as modernizations of modernities. However, before I attempt to apply Beck's (1994) model to this end, it should be made clear that he does not share the historical interpretation presented in this book. Alongside his innovative thinking on contemporary modernity, he maintains a traditional social theory interpretation of the historical modern: the 'simple modernity' that reflexive modernity is superseding in his model is industrial. Hence risk society is contrasted throughout by 'industrial society' viewed in a quite conventional manner. No doubt this relates to Beck's overall purpose to update social theory to contemporary circumstances, but it does mean that traditional social theory is not challenged for its historical veracity in his work. Despite his reference to 'many modernities', this is not given historical expression so that Beck's work certainly does not suggest the existence of a modernity prior to industrialization.

Three historical modernities means there are two shifts, from mercantile to industrial and from the latter to consumer modernity. My purpose is to see whether change by stealth reflecting the success of each old order is a reasonable way to view the two changes to new modernities. The change in thinking this entails should not be underestimated. In Beck's words, there is a 'taboo' to be broken on treating the immanence of change in society seriously:

> The idea that the transition from one epoch to another could take place unintended and unpolitically, bypassing all forums for political decisions, the lines of conflict and the partisan controversies, contradicts the democratic self-understanding of this society just as much as it does the fundamental convictions of its sociology. (Beck, 1994, p. 3)

This concern intersects with the division between 'Braudellian' history with its focus on everyday lives and orthodox histories that have emphasized 'high' political events. Braudel's (1980) work is known for its depiction of long-term structures – economic, social, cultural – and the resulting slow societal changes. I will be concerned with Braudel's 'slow history' of unintended changes in periods when it seems to have 'speeded up': even *longues durées* are not for ever, they change with epochs.

The first shift in modernity occurred between the Dutch and British hegemonies in the eighteenth century. The great social optimism of the hegemonic Dutch in the mid-seventeenth century gave way to a national obsession with decline in the eighteenth century (Jacob and Mijnhardt, 1992). But beyond the Netherlands the mercantilist system it did so much to create continued to prosper in the wake of English–French rivalries: the 'crisis of the seventeenth century' (of which the Dutch were the great exception) was not repeated in the next century. Nevertheless, there was an uncertainty about where society was going. Enlightenment ideas about progress remained highly abstract and agricultural improvement remained localized. What future for a system reliant on slavery in the Americas and plunder in India to generate great wealth? It is known through hindsight that this mercantile system was to be overwhelmed in the nineteenth century by industrialization and that the new society was embryonic in England in the second half of the eighteenth century: this change is called the industrial revolution.

Of course, the industrial revolution is conventionally interpreted as the transition from tradition to modernity, the economic face of change to be placed in harness with the French Revolution representing political change. From the perspective adopted here this standard pairing is problematic. The early years of industrialization in England were first designated a revolution by the French for the explicit purpose of linking economic and technical changes to their own political upheavals. Given the modern interpretation of a revolution (i.e. change that does *not* finish where it begins), the political events in France in 1789 certainly warrant the heroic title of revolution, but can the same be said for the economic changes in England that occurred between 1760 and 1840? Obviously most people have answered in the affirmative because of the tremendous effects of these decades of change. The effects are not in dispute, but why call it a revolution in particular? What seems to be happening is that a shift in modernity as a process which is surreptitious, unplanned, unintended and unpolitical, to use Beck's (1994) terms, is being dressed up in the language of politics to make it explicable to the new world it has created. Despite the litany of inventor/entrepreneur 'heroes' that is found in the standard accounts of the industrial revolution, it is relatively easy to show that the processes described conform much more closely to Beck's model of change than to any theory of revolution. This was a process that was geographically isolated from the high politics of London and most certainly did not feature in the court versus country politics of the times. There was no plan to create an industrial society or a new modern world, the 'heroes' were men with local initiatives that could be, and were, largely ignored by the powers that be. But they were fulfilling the immanent potential of mercantile modernity by adding a new production dimension that would, ultimately, fundamentally change all social relations within and beyond their contemporary modern world-system.

The changes that occurred between British and American hegemony about a century ago are not usually given the accolade of the title of revolution but the fundamental shift is well documented. The same combination of economic and political successes combined with cultural consternation is to be found. One reason for the lack of recognition as a social transition seems to be that the changes have been viewed separately in their different spheres and are not seen as a single package of processes in the manner in which the industrial revolution is viewed. Here is a list of the familiar changes: global closure in international politics (no more land for imperial expansion), global communication (steamship postal services and undersea cables), petroleum and the internal combustion engine (cars, trucks and aeroplanes), delivery of electricity to cities for homes and factories, corporate mergers creating an oligarchic capitalism, new management techniques for mass production, and all celebrated by the art of the modernist movement. To different degrees these were linked to a shift towards the USA as the new beacon of modernity: according to Temperley (1976, pp. 332–4), it was at this time that the image of America becomes 'the land of the future'; for Americans Britain becomes a place of nostalgia, replacing its earlier location as their land of the future.

The crucial 'silent' shift in the logic of everyday life occurred after 1880 in American cities with the rise of a consumption ethic for urban professionals indexed by the establishment of a national advertising industry (Fox and Lears, 1983, p. xi). The old work ethic was replaced by a 'new morality' consisting of 'new ideals of self-fulfilment and immediate gratification' (p. xii). Lears describes the transition as follows:

> In the United States, as elsewhere, the bourgeois ethos had enjoined perpetual work, compulsive saving, civic responsibility, and a rigid morality of self-denial. By the early twentieth century that outlook had begun to give way to a new set of values sanctioning periodic leisure, compulsive spending, apolitical passivity, and an apparently permissive (but subtly coercive) morality of individual fulfilment. The older culture was suited to a production-orientated society of small entrepreneurs; the newer culture epitomized a consumption-orientated society dominated by bureaucratic corporations. (Lear, 1983, p. 3)

This seems to me to be a classic case of Beck's (1994) model of small changes having large cumulative effects and thus justifies dividing his 'industrial society' into two modernities. By the 1920s Los Angeles was showing the way forward with a completely new urban structure – a metropolis of suburbs – based upon the motor car (Fishman, 1987). It was at this time that Gramsci was to ask whether America was beginning 'a new historical epoch' (Hoare and Smith, 1971, p. 277). The post-1945 rise of consumer society and the spread of popular affluence as a consequence of American hegemony have shown that the answer to Gramsci's question is yes.

Consensus and coercion in the projection of hegemonic power

Jim Blaut (1987; 1993) has taught that it is necessary to be very careful with the idea of global diffusion models. The assumption that modernity, however conceptualized, would be the 'great unifier' creating the world as a single homogenized space has not materialized. To begin with, places 'receiving modernity' have not been as placid as the diffusion model requires. More generally, there is a geohistory of modernities: becoming modern is negotiated in different ways in different places at different times. Thus modernity has been marked as much by variety as by uniformity. This unevenness or 'patchiness' of modernity has been a recent concern of Goran Therborn (1995), who identifies four distinctive 'passes of entry' through which modernity has spread. These are the 'European gate of revolution or reform', the 'new worlds of the Americas', modernization induced by 'external threat', and the 'gate of the colonial zone'. While a major advance on simple diffusion models, Therborn's approach continues to treat what is being spread, the modernity, in the singular. Here I will loosely merge his idea of gateways with the prime modernities model.

I will begin by reducing Therborn's patchiness of modernity to its minimal expression, the core–periphery pattern of the world-economy. Since the hegemon is part of the core it might be expected that its relation to other core states is different from the way it relates to the non-core. Basically consensus has dominated inter-core hegemonic relations, while coercion typifies relations beyond the core. This pattern was set in train politically immediately world war was ended. At the peace-making the victorious hegemons made no territorial claims within Europe: at Westphalia in 1648, at Vienna in 1815 and at Yalta and Potsdam in 1945, European boundaries were redrawn but without the Dutch, British or Americans gaining any territorial benefit. Beyond Europe, however, it was another matter, especially with regard to strategic locations. The result in each case was that substituting a peace for world war in Europe was accompanied by many 'little wars' in other parts of the world.

The critical process through which hegemons influenced fellow members of the core was emulation: because each hegemon is indisputably a great success story in its path to high hegemony, its rivals try to emulate them in processes commonly known as mercantilism, industrialization and Americanization. This is what is meant by hegemonic 'intellectual and moral leadership' at the world-system scale. But there is a major geographical difference between Gramsci's original concept of hegemony and the more recent widespread use of world hegemony. In changing the hegemonic agent from a social class to a prescient state and its civil society, the definitional basis of conceiving 'moral and intellectual leadership' changes fundamentally. From a geohistorical perspective the crucial point is that a hegemonic state, unlike a hegemonic class, is defined as a place. This makes it much more concrete; you can visit a hegemonic state. But what do visitors see? The meaning of a hegemonic place is more than the usual sovereign territory and national homeland; it is a special place which expresses the future today. Non-coercive leadership is based upon social emulation and the crucial stimulus for this process is a representation of hegemonic social organization as the future for all others. Not emulating means 'falling behind', not keeping up with the latest and best, that is, not remaining modern. It is in this sense that the hegemon is viewed as the most modern of the moderns.

This place-interpretation of hegemony is a direct challenge to the idea that the process of modernization, by destroying communities, obliterates places from the experience of modernity. Hegemony provides, perhaps, the best example of Agnew's (1987) basic contention that modernity not only destroys old places but constructs new places to replace them. In the case of the Dutch, the image of success was Amsterdam harbour with its hundreds of ships waiting to unload their commodities. Emulation meant recreating 'new Amsterdams' in other lands in the restructuring we know as mercantilism. Although the most successful emulators were England and France, the most explicit place creation in this mercantile modernity was, of course, Peter the Great's construction of St Petersburg as Russia's 'window on the west'. In the case of the British, the images of success were the great cotton mills of Lancashire producing textiles for the world. This new modern place attracted visitors from across Europe and the USA to find out how to create 'new Manchesters' in their own lands. This emulation is known as industrialization and the most successful initially were north-eastern USA and the German Rhinelands; for the latter a new word, *Manchesterthum*, was devised, emphasizing its place origins (Briggs, 1963, p. 106). In the case of American hegemony, the image of success is suburbia, first epitomized by Los Angeles, where consumption was enjoyed well away from the making of commodities. And there was no need to visit this place to view its workings – American suburbia visited the rest of the world first in cinema and subsequently on TV to stimulate Americanization and create consumer modernity. Suburbanization around cities and towns across the world is today's conspicuous example of a modernization creating new places. Representing hegemons as special places of the future gives them a massive cultural power which is, I think, still not fully appreciated.

However, viewed across the whole system, the emulation of hegemonic practices has been a very limited affair. It can be interpreted as core-making or core renewal in the development of the modern world-system. Hence it is a means for defining the core zone within each hegemonic cycle, the spatial core of a new modernity. For emulation to affect another civil society deeply requires a certain level of cultural similarity or some other unusual enabling situation to exist. This has meant that successful emulation that embodies the full fruits of a new modernity has been a relatively localized process. In the Dutch case only England and France emerged as mercantilist powers to rival the Dutch although Sweden, Denmark and Brandenburg-Prussia also embarked upon foreign mercantilist endeavours. From Britain in the nineteenth century, industrialization spread initially only to define a north Atlantic core. The consumer culture of Americanization in the second half of the twentieth century has overwhelmed Western Europe and Japan. There is little or no coercion in this process – Americanization of France has been called 'seducing the French' (Kuisel, 1993) – since these are societies able and willing to keep up to date with the latest modernity.

Core-making is complemented by periphery-making. Beyond the core, modernity has arrived through coercion. This can be thought of as operating through two processes: threat and force. In the first case a section of the political elites in a country respond to external threat by instigating a state revolution and coercing their populace to the new ways. Peter the Great's reorganization of Russia represents a classic example of this process as he tried to bring the new mercantile modernity to his realm. The Meiji Restoration in Japan represents the most successful example of industrial modernity being imposed from above, but there were other less successful state revolutions with similar goals, notably in China and Turkey. The revolutions that brought the Cold War to a conclusion represent the imposition of consumer modernity through external threat. By the 1980s it was clear that COMECON had failed because it had created an economy that was simply out of date, meaning it could not produce the consumer commodities at the heart of contemporary modernity. But more on this most important recent example later in chapter 5; here I need just note that all three modernities have spread beyond the core through perceived external threat

stimulating the overturning of failing states which were considered
to be irredeemably out of date.

Use of force to spread modernity is as old as modernity itself.
Colony-creation peaked in the seventeenth and nineteenth centuries
as two cycles of imperialism which overlap broadly with the first
two hegemonic cycles (Taylor, 1993a). This imposition of modernities through conquest creates a very small colonial elite who benefit
from the restructuring of territory to meet new world-economy needs
through coercive exploitation of labour. 'Plantation America' extending from north-east Brazil through the West Indies to Mary-
land represents imperial experience of mercantile modernity. The
so-called 'age of imperialism' from 1870 globalized the old Atlantic
economy to create a great peripheral supply zone of agricultural
goods and raw materials for servicing the new industrial modernity established throughout the core by the turn of the century. Every
colony had its role to play: Britain received gold and diamonds
from South Africa, coffee from Kenya, tea from Ceylon, cotton
from the Sudan, cocoa from the Gold Coast, rubber from Malaya,
hemp from Bengal, sugar from Jamaica, and so on. In contrast to
the above, American hegemony has witnessed the completion of
decolonization so that military conquest has not been a feature of
the era of consumer modernity. This does not mean, of course, that
coercion has not been a prime feature for the newly designated
'third world'. The initial post-colonial theories of benign modernization soon succumbed to a reality of military states targeting their
weapons on their own peoples. Why this should have happened
can be derived from the poverty of the modernization theories themselves. Basically they conflated industrial and consumer modernities into one process. This meant that attempts to industrialize,
with varying degrees of success, occurred not in the context of the
frugal bourgeois saving regime of nineteenth-century Europe but,
rather, with the consumer mentality of twentieth-century America.
The result has been to produce the most unequal state-societies
created within the modern world-system. Combining core levels of
consumption with mass poverty has produced societies such as
Brazil's, sometimes referred to as Belgium plus Bangladesh. But
even poorer countries have not missed out on new ostentatious
consumptions. There has been what I call the Muhammad Ali
effect. Just before the advent of satellite TV, all the major world

heavyweight fights took place, not in the USA, but in third world countries where the really rich lived and were willing to pay top dollar for the ultimate consumption, world heavyweight championship boxing. Hence New York's Madison Square Garden and Las Vegas's Caesar's Palace had to give way to the Philippines (the 'thriller in Manila', Ali v. Frazier), Jamaica (Frazier v. Foreman), Malaysia (Ali v. Bugner) and, most famously of all, in the kleptocracy of Zaire (the 'rumble in the jungle', Ali v. Foreman). Such has been the distorted consumer modernity of the third world.

3

Ordinary Modernity

Prime modernities are distinctive but, importantly, are also related: I have presented them as cumulative, as stages in the development of the modern world-system. Whilst the last chapter delineated their differences, in this chapter I concentrate upon one key dimension of their similarities. In doing so I identify a generic link across all three modernities which I shall term ordinary modernity. The innovative capacity of the civil societies of hegemonic states has not been limited to new political economies; they have invented new socio-cultural representations. It is quite remarkable the way in which the Dutch, the British and the Americans have pioneered new art forms which, despite the separation of centuries, exhibit a common thread celebrating ordinariness. This is, of course, a symptom of the distinctive nature of social relations within hegemonic states. I shall use innovative art forms as a clue for discovering the similarities between the prime modernities as three expressions of ordinary modernity.

The creative arts have traditionally been sponsored by the state and the great. With hegemons this has been much less the case, with sponsors replaced by markets. This has meant that, collectively, ordinary consumers have been economically more powerful than the state and the great in the art worlds of hegemons. The result of such unusual circumstances has been that popular art forms have been created which represent ordinary people within the societies they depict. This is the communality that exists across three hegemonic cycles over four centuries. Each hegemon's civil society has been exceptionally innovative in creating new art forms for new markets. These are Dutch genre painting, the English novel and American popular cinema. Despite the immense differences in media, the communality is that the everyday lives of ordinary people have been made a particular focus of attention in each.

Celebrating the ordinary is historically very rare. The vast majority of art celebrates the great and the transcendent as part of the ideological legitimation of the ruling strata. That hegemons do not follow this custom is crucial to understanding the social meaning of hegemony and the nature of the modernity it promotes.

Cultural celebrations of ordinariness

The culture of absolutism is the baroque, early modern European 'high culture' in which an elaborate artistic symbolism glorified church and king. Originating in Italian church architecture intended to replicate heaven on earth, kings soon discovered the power of such cultural artefacts to impress rivals and subjects alike. Louis XIV's magnificent palace at Versailles remains the greatest monument of absolutism. From today's perspective this is 'tourist Europe', the world of magnificent cities and palaces – what Nussbaum (1953, p. 30) has called the 'holy places of European culture'. This grand European style permeated all high culture, going beyond architecture to 'classical' music, heroic sculptures and glorious paintings. But there was one country that stayed outside the 'High Tradition': the baroque had little to offer the Dutch (Huizinga, 1968, pp. 11–12). This does not mean a Philistine or 'uncultured' United Provinces, quite the opposite: the Dutch invented a unique 'little tradition', a counter-baroque style (Mukerji, 1983, p. 78).

The greatest Dutch cultural achievements in the seventeenth century were in painting, where a new style of representation was developed. In contrast to baroque symbolism illustrating a decisive moment in a narrative, Dutch 'genre' painters portrayed scenes from the world they lived in (Fuchs, 1978, pp. 45–6). Israel describes it thus:

The art and artists of the Golden Age captured the whole of the physical, social and cultural reality surrounding the Dutch burgher of the day, depicting his own household and civic world, the rural surroundings, and also what surrounded that – the soldiers on the landward side, and ships and the sea on the other. (Israel, 1995, p. 562)

It is this 'realism' that marks off Dutch painting as special (Fuchs, 1978, pp. 40–1). As an art it attempted to mirror the facts of life as they existed by drawing directly on the artist's visual experiences of his surroundings. For instance, unlike the other great 'masters' of the period, Rembrandt did not visit Rome to enhance his artistic sensibilities, a feature he shared with many less esteemed Dutch artists (Levey, 1969, p. 9; Fuchs, 1978, p. 43). The result was that, in Fuchs's (1978, p. 62) words, the new realism originated from the 'context of the optimistic contemplation of one's own world'. There could hardly be a greater contrast with baroque painting; instead of glorifying the great, the ordinary are celebrated.

It is important to understand the context in which this new art emerged. Gombrich (1989, p. 88) writes of 'a crisis of art' in northern Europe in the wake of the Reformation. Protestant Europe's suspicion of idolatry took away the artist's stock in trade, the devotional picture. Although a few artists were able to find work in the courts of princes as portrait painters '[t]here was only one Protestant country in Europe where art fully survived the crisis of the Reformation – that was the Netherlands' (Gombrich, 1989, p. 295). Instead of waiting for commissions, artists in the United Provinces painted to sell, thus creating the first art market. In this competitive context artists specialized in certain types or 'genres' of paintings so as to achieve a specific reputation in the market place. In short, painting became an industry with middle men, the first art dealers, supplying people from a wide range of occupations with a new commodity to consume. The size of the resulting market was quite astounding: one estimate puts the number of paintings in Holland in 1650 at two and a half million (Israel, 1995, p. 555).

According to Nussbaum (1953, p. 50) genre artists 'made a vision of the world in the prosaic terms of the new bourgeois, without royalty and without religion, even without more philosophy than a comfortable bourgeois acceptance of solidity and luxury'.

The paintings can be interpreted at two levels. First, if, as Price (1974, p. 119) says, 'the roots' of Dutch artistic originality 'lay in the nature of seventeenth century Dutch society', the paintings should provide a visual insight into Dutch society. From group portraits of satisfied burghers to scenes of ordinary working people, the ruled in the United Provinces are visible, when elsewhere only the rulers could be seen. For instance, Fuchs (1978, p. 41) describes one of Jan Steen's paintings as showing 'an ordinary interior with ordinary people', which is typical of the domestic genre of which Steen was a master. Second, the meaning of particular painting can be decoded; why topics are painted and what it tells about the nature of the society. Among the various genres, one is particularly interesting in this respect: still-life composition, which Gombrich (1989, p. 339) calls 'the most "specialised" branch of Dutch painting'. They are interesting for my argument for two reasons. First, as simple paintings of a group of ordinary items, they show just how far removed Dutch culture was from the baroque. In the latter, the subjects of the great paintings were major episodes from the Bible or some equally revered topic. In contrast the Dutch created masterpieces from the most trivial of subjects. Second, although the subjects may have been trivial, they were not chosen arbitrarily but reflected the new comforts of Dutch bourgeois society. Typically, still-lives showed 'beautiful vessels filled with wine and appetising fruit, or other dainties arranged on lovely china' (Gombrich, 1989, p. 339; Price, 1974, p. 123). They were painted to be hung in the dining rooms of Dutch homes as permanent 'reminders of the joys of the table' (Gombrich, 1989, p. 339). No wonder this genre of paintings sold so well in the new popular art market of the Netherlands.

A very different popular market emerged in eighteenth-century Britain commonly known as the rise of the reading public. To quote Dr Johnson, Britain became 'a nation of readers' in a new 'age of authors' (Watt, 1972, pp. 40 and 64). In London, alone, the number of printers increased from just 70 in 1724 to 372 by 1802, producing newspapers, magazines, pamphlets and books (1972, p. 48). One notable feature was the tendency 'for literature to become a primarily feminine pursuit' (p. 10). This was the result of increasing numbers of middle-class households in which the women of the family had much time on their hands for leisure pursuits. Nobody knows how much the growth of the publications market was due to women but the development of the novel as a new product suggests that they were important. In any case the English novel played a role analogous to genre paintings in Britain's celebration of the ordinary.

As a form of fiction, the novel is undoubtedly 'modern': it was an English invention of the eighteenth century and use of the term 'novel' to describe this form of story telling was established only at the end of that century (Watt, 1972, p. 10). Unlike more traditional story telling, the novel aspired to be realistic and Ian Watt (1972, p. 14) uses this to draw parallels with philosophical realism. The term realism was first used in France in the 1830s with reference to Rembrandt's paintings as imitations of reality. Watt traces modern realism to another Dutch source, the intellectual refugees Descartes and Locke. This triple Dutch connection is quite suggestive. I will interpret the novel as the British cultural invention for celebrating the ordinary.

A crucial point about the novel was that it eschewed mythology and legend as traditional sources of stories and instead produced original 'storylines'. Traditional stories drew their audience into an unchanging world of customs; the novel took an individualistic turn and, since any individual's experience is always unique, the story is always new. Hence Watt (1972, p. 14) notes, the novel 'is well-named'. Every novel is about particular people in particular circumstances with definite time and place contexts. In short, it is a literary vehicle for an ever-changing world which is why it is quintessentially modern, a feature of the modern world-system. It reaches its apogee as a cultural influence in Britain during its hegemony in the great era of the Victorian novel.

In a remarkable flourishing of an art form, the following great novelists, who were to dominate world literature in the mid-nineteenth century, were all born in the decade of the 1810s in England: William Thackeray, Charles Dickens, Anthony Trollope, Charlotte and Emily Brontë, George Eliot and Charles Kingsley (W. Allen, 1958, p. 139). Allen (p. 145) describes their collective contribution thus: 'Sharing the preoccupations of their times rooted in the popular life of their age, they produced an art that was truly national.' But it was 'national' only in the sense that the British nation was middle class because 'It was the respectable who composed the great reading public, and it was for the respectable that the great Victorian novelists wrote' (p. 145). This idea of respectability was at the heart of English novel writing. It was the way the middle class separated themselves from a dissolute aristocracy on the one hand and an ill-disciplined working class on the other. T. B. Tomlinson (1976, p. 14) calls the early nineteenth-century English novel 'very much a middle class enterprise' because it incorporated bourgeois interests within its plots while generally omitting much else that was happening. The high politics of Napoleon and Wellington are missing from the English novel as are the radical politics of the Luddites. As with modernity projects in other contexts, a more stable world is provided, in this case as the background for the private middle-class lives that make up the story (Tomlinson, 1976, p. 15).

This relatively safe 'ordinary world' has been reproduced in the twentieth century through the American cinema. For instance, according to Russell Taylor (1982, p. 84) cinema-goers across the world could forget the cares of the world: 'In the magical sanctuary of the cinema you could have been forgiven for supposing that the most important issue in the world was whether Doris Day would succeed . . . in preserving her virginity until wedding bells at the final fade-out.' It was not just that America's great cultural contribution to the modern world has been in the cinema, it is the fact that they made popular movies which is important. While Europeans developed a reputation for 'highbrow' films for the few, Americans produced films for everyone.

The resulting domination of this media has been described by John Lukacs (1993, p. 273) with elegant simplicity: 'As early as 1925, millions of people in Europe knew the names and faces of American movie stars while they knew not the name of their own prime minister.' In the 1930s Hollywood provided escapism from poverty, with its glittering stars and spectacular films. After being harnessed to the war effort in the early 1940s, the last years of the decade were a time of major changes. Anti-trust legislation ended studio control of outlets and anti-communist witch-hunts eliminated any artistic radicalism. Cinema audiences in the USA peaked in 1946 and, although the export market remained buoyant, the coming threat of TV was hanging over the industry. The new suburban lifestyles that were growing rapidly in the post-war years favoured the home entertainment TV offered in competition with films shown on cinemas in far away downtown. This problem was overcome in the 1950s by the Hollywood studios through producing for TV: the age of the 'fifty minute featurette' had arrived (Lloyd, 1986, p. 230).

All this added up to the safe and bland films typifying the 1950s. Although various old film genres dominate critical discussion – westerns, musicals, war, gangster, horror, science fiction, etc. – it is another type of film which tells more about America at this time. The stock-in-trade movies of the 1950s hardly qualify as a genre at all: domestic films – simple comedies and lightweight dramas, some drawn from early successes of TV series – were produced in their hundreds. These are interesting, not for their quality, but for the taken-for-granted world they portray. As Taylor (1982, p. 84) observes: 'As the fifties progressed, the movies showed American life becoming more secure, cosy and domestic.' This is the same bourgeois domesticity to be found in Dutch genre paintings and the English novel: these were stories of ordinary people living comfortable lives – for much of the rest of the world it was the American dream on celluloid.

There was one important innovation in 1950s American cinema: teen films. A new youth culture was one product of America's affluent society. Ordinary young people constituted a sizeable market for the first time in history and the new consumers were given a new name – teenagers. Teenage became equated with 'leisure, pleasure and conspicuous consumption' (Lloyd, 1986, p. 244). Hollywood was only too pleased to cater for this new market with a string of films including rock and roll features, teenage/school love stories and holiday/beach movies. Above all these films represented the ordinary concerns of youth, adolescent worries that were timeless but had never previously been commercialized.

Not only the films changed, so too did the stars. In the old Hollywood star system, the leading actors and actresses were promoted by the studio publicity machines to be demi-gods. In contrast the 1950s have been termed 'the great period of the star-as-ordinary-person' (Lloyd, 1986, p. 253). The stars came down to earth, as the saying goes, and instead of being promoted as superhuman, they were presented to their audiences as 'straightforward, uncomplicated average human beings' (p. 253), the boy or girl next door. In Ann Lloyd's (1986, p. 253) words: 'stars like Doris Day, Rock Hudson, June Allyson and Gregory Peck insisted that the everyday was best.' And the everyday was American middle-class home life in the comfort of suburbia.

Feeling comfortable: the modern home

The point about the last section was not that the hegemons dominated the 'high cultures' of their eras but that they each excelled in a particular sphere with a common social meaning. Ordinariness as cultural expression is premised upon the social practices of ordinary modernity. The time has come to define the latter in contrast to other general interpretations of modernity.

As discussed in chapter 1, modernity is an ambiguous, multifaceted concept and this has allowed different features to be promoted as core characteristics. Most commonly, its 'rationality' is emphasized especially in historical arguments: being rational lay behind the scientific revolution of the seventeenth century, provided the cutting edge for the Enlightenment in the eighteenth century, and created the technology of the nineteenth century that made universal progress seem so inevitable. Recently, Anthony Giddens (1990), with his eye firmly focused on contemporary globalization, has argued that modernity depends upon new relations of trust. All world-systems separate everyday life experiences from important determinants that are system-wide but the modern world-system deals with this separation distinctively. Whereas pre-modern societies treated 'extra-local' effects in terms of divine providence, under modernity such risks are dealt with through trust in ordered systems of social relations that operate to integrate local practices into the system. The contemporary explosion of reliance on 'plastic' money, for instance, is only possible because of widespread trust in the system that operates this banking innovation. But both the philosophers' and historians' arguments for rationality and the sociologists' and economists' arguments for trust are 'top-down' interpretations of modernity that are far removed from what I term ordinary modernity. I argue that studying modernity should not neglect the fact that modern society is self-consciously modern. To do so is to produce only a partial appreciation of what it is to be modern. The popularity of modernity in the twentieth century has been crucial, not only for sustaining modernity, but also in influencing the changing nature of modernity. So is there a single concept, like rationality or trust, to capture the essence of ordinary modernity? I think there is and I offer comfort as my candidate for the concept to take on this onerous role.

What does it mean to elevate the commonplace notion of comfort to be a core concept of modernity? Like rationality and trust, once comfort is examined seriously it turns out to be a very complex idea. Witold Rybczynski (1986, p. 231) writes of the 'mystery of comfort' because it is impossible to measure it objectively: 'it may be enough to realise that domestic comfort involves a range of attributes – convenience, efficiency, leisure, ease, pleasure, domesticity, intimacy, and privacy – all of which contribute to the experience; common sense will do the rest.' But, of course, this common sense is only common to modern society. In the invention of medieval society as a foil for modernity, pre-modern settings may have been romantically enchanting but they were never viewed as comfortable (Cantor, 1991). Every suburbanite appreciates that her or his life has a degree of comfort unattainable in medieval Europe, even for a king and queen in their (draughty) castle. Of course, knowledge of sumptuous lifestyles in other civilizations, both classical Rome and the great oriental empires, is part of modern historical consciousness but it is understood that these extreme images of comfort were enjoyed by the very few, a very small elite living off the backs of the many. Modern comfort, in contrast, is available to the ordinary man and woman, the descendants of serfs and slaves not kings and emperors. Modernity, therefore, is for ordinary people.

The pre-eminent comfortable modern place is the home. This is what lies behind the hall, the small entry room where the stairs begin and outdoor clothes are hung in the typical contemporary house. Of course, medieval houses of the nobility and merchants famously had their halls but these were very different, dominating the whole house. These contrasting house arrangements represent two completely different worlds. The great halls of the past were multiple-use spaces that were essentially public in nature: a place for transacting business, for cooking and eating, for entertainment and for sleeping at night (Rybczynski, 1986, p. 25). Today, the hall has been reduced to a small transition zone between a private home and a public outside. It is the modern home's frontier, the zone for entering and leaving and where visitors are dealt with. Although important for providing a home's initial image to the outside world, the hall does not have to be comfortable like other rooms because it is not a place where people are expected to stay for long. If the visitors are friends they may be invited beyond the hall to specialized rooms that are prized for their comfort and convenience – living room or lounge, dining room, kitchen, bathroom and bedrooms. It is this private space of the home that is an essential locus of ordinary modernity.

This modernity beyond the hall had to be created and the three hegemons are intimately implicated in the invention of the modern home and making it comfortable. The modern sense of the word comfort came into usage only in the eighteenth century but the development of the modern home precedes this language development. According to Rybczynski (1986, p. 51), 'there was one place where seventeenth century domestic interior evolved in a way that was arguably unique, and that can be described as having been, at the very least, exemplary.' This was, of course, the Dutch Republic where economic successes were accompanied by new cultural behaviours. Dutch merchants were family-orientated and lived in small households with few or no servants. Children were integral to the new family life and instead of being apprenticed stayed at home and attended school. In this way the Dutch invented what today is understood as childhood (Rybczynski, 1986, p. 60). New town houses were built or converted to adapt to these new practices and therefore eliminated the traditional mix of work with residency. The ground floor was still treated as a public space to entertain visitors but the upper floors were a special family place. Friends allowed access to the upstairs were required to remove their street shoes so as not to disrupt the cleanliness of the home. This boundary between public and private spaces was the new idea which enabled houses to become homes (1986, p. 66). Here the Dutch could express their personal likes and dislikes to fit individual family needs such as decorating their walls with paintings. A contemporary English critic of the Netherlands, Sir William Temple, after noting the propensity for monetary tightness among the Dutch, gives one exception: expenditure on furniture and other commodities for the home (p. 61). All in all, the Dutch produced the first modern homes in the world, cosy settings for the family life of ordinary people.

In the eighteenth century, interior comfort advanced in two forms. In France aristocratic and royal tastes were converted into sumptuous fashions for palaces. In more bourgeois England where the Hanoverian court had little cultural influence (Colley, 1992), a simpler comfort was developed for the country houses of the middle classes. This Georgian style is a fashion that refuses to become out of date because of its suitability for comfortable home-life. This was the era of Chippendale chairs and the ubiquitous diffusion of the 'Windsor chair', both popular because they were so easy to sit in (Rybczynski, 1986, pp. 115–16). English economic successes provided the enabling wealth for new cultural practices related to leisure and the home became the locus of card games, dinner parties, various entertainments such as billiards and dances and, of course, it was where the latest novels were read. Rybczynski (1986, p. 112) thinks it highly relevant that Jane Austen so frequently used the words 'comfort' and 'comfortable' in what he describes as her 'domestic genre of novel writing' focusing on the homelife of England's middle classes. She even coins the phrase 'English comfort' as two words that seemed naturally to go together. In fact it was the English who brought carpets down from the walls to make floors quieter and nicer to walk on. They even introduced the fashion for wall-to-wall carpeting. But their main contribution to domestic comfort was to bring furniture out from the walls. It is with the eighteenth-century English that the arrangement of sofas and easy chairs around the fireplace, the epitome of warm cosiness, makes its appearance in the home (Rybczynski, 1986, p. 118). It is this 'English taste' that spread through Europe and America as ordinary homes with their many personal 'knick-knacks' became the hallmark of the 'Victorian age' (Briggs, 1988).

However, there is a major 'comfort gap' between nineteenth-century 'English comfort' and today's expectations of comfort. Lighting, heating and plumbing lagged behind furniture in the development of the home. For most of the eighteenth century artificial lighting still came from wax candles and, although new oil lamps appeared by 1800, it was not until the 1840s that gas lighting in homes became popular. But gas lighting was dirty and added to the smoky atmosphere created by poorly fumed fires. There were many inventions to try to make the home more efficient but they all foundered on one key stumbling block: the lack of access to power in a form small enough for domestic needs. Comfort depended upon servants until the introduction of the small electric motor.

The introduction of electricity into the home illustrates well the transition from British to American cultural leadership. The first domestic light bulbs were invented independently in Britain and the USA in 1877 by Joseph Swan and Thomas Edison respectively. But there the similarity ended. In 1880 Swan's invention was used to light up Cragside, the Northumbrian home of the Newcastle industrialist Lord Armstrong, the first house to have electric lights (Rybczynski, 1986, pp. 150–1). This was exceptional, however. By now social support for such innovation was disappearing in England; Rybczynski writes of 'a curious situation' in England whereby modern conveniences came to be seen as vulgar. In contrast, by 1882 Edison had laid electric cables in part of New York so that 200 houses were using 5,000 Edison bulbs for their lighting (Rybczynski, 1986, p. 150). This was the lead the rest of the world followed and by 1900 major cities throughout the USA and Europe had electric companies supplying current through underground cables. Once such distribution networks were in place, 'home appliances' could be produced with electric motors to finally extend comfort from domestic leisure to domestic work – what Rybczynski (1986, p. 158) refers to as 'the great American innovation in the home'. As early as 1893, an 'electric kitchen' was exhibited at the Chicago World Fair and very soon a large range of appliances was widely available from such well-known companies as Westinghouse and Hoover. Irons, vacuum cleaners, washing machines, sewing machines, fans, toasters, cookers, hotplates – convenience came to the home, especially the American home. By the middle of the 1920s over 60 per cent of American houses had electricity and this constituted more than half the world market (Rybczynski, 1986, p. 153). It was this scale of operation that reduced the price of electricity, which stimulated the market for appliances and which used more electricity, creating a spiralling market. Hence domesticity was at the forefront of the USA developing the first mass consumption society. But with all this convenience, basic comfort was never forgotten: it is America that invented the bathroom as a three-fixture space of bath, water closet and hand basin (Rybczynski, 1986,

p. 164). This ubiquitous place of ordinary luxury illustrates how far modernity has improved the lives of millions of people in the twentieth century.

Ordinary modernity as comfort was therefore a product of hegemonic civil societies where wealth was accumulated and distributed widely enough to create new domestic worlds. To a large extent the process was cumulative as bourgeois influence spread throughout the modern world-system. But the three hegemonic episodes in this development were very different in their geographies. In particular, the Dutch and the British created new homes in very different locales: small town houses and Georgian country houses respectively. America's contribution to ordinary modernity was specifically designed to marry these two geographies: suburbia integrated conveniences of urban life with the atmosphere of country life. But suburbia is much more than a blend of past locales. It represents a distinctive new geographical phenomenon, spaces of concentrated comfort. The Dutch and British contributions to ordinary modernity focused at the level of the house, American suburbia is many such houses in a homogeneous environment of comfort writ large.

Suburbia: the domestic landscape of consumer modernity

In strictly geographical terms the existence of suburbs is as old as urban growth. Indeed, residential growth on the edge of the city was distinctive in pre-modern urban development but its characteristics were the opposite of the modern suburb. Pre-modern suburbs were for urban outcasts, they were dens of iniquity outside respectable urban society. In contrast, the modern suburb is designed to be pre-eminently respectable. This is a classic example of a modern reality completely subverting its historical antecedent. Suburbia is a special place for family living that takes homes out of a corrupting urban influence and relocates them in new communities with rural settings. The classic modern suburb consists of single family houses in large gardens set back from tree-lined roads. Perhaps the key feature is the front lawn, which is a private space that has a public function (Fishman, 1987, pp. 146–7). Maintained by the homeowner, its effect is a communal one: by separating houses from their road, the sequence of green front lawns converts an urban street into a country lane to produce the ideal suburban landscape.

Although, significantly, American writers believe the modern suburb to be a US invention, Robert Fishman (1987, p. 116) has shown that its origins may be traced back to the growth of eighteenth-century London. Beginning as high-class suburbs, this urban form was converted into a general middle-class residential zone in mid-nineteenth-century Manchester where new wealth was used to move out of the industrial city. This produced the first example of the now familiar urban structure of working-class inner city and middle-class outer city famously described by Engels in 1844. The British invented the suburb as an exclusionary zone, therefore. The American contribution was to popularize the idea of the suburb as a goal for every family. This notion of 'suburbs for all' can be found as early as 1868 although it is only with the coming of the 'affluent society' in the twentieth century that it achieved widespread credibility (Fishman, 1987, p. 129). Americans did not eliminate exclusion from suburbia, of course, but they produced gradations of exclusion so that there were different suburbs for different family budgets. This culminated in the 1950s as the decade of greatest suburban growth in US history; the 1960 census recorded an additional 19 million people living in the country's suburbs since 1950 (Hall, 1988, p. 294).

Large-scale suburbanization began in the late nineteenth century in both Britain and the USA as a result of improvements in urban transport. But the geographical outcome was far from satisfactory: the resulting railway and streetcar suburbs created narrow, linear patterns of growth in the outer city combined with massive congestion in the city centre. The motor car created the means to break away from this urban structure by enabling suburbia to invade all available spaces and hence to dominate the modern city. Los Angeles, the 'suburban metropolis' as Fishman (1987, chapter 6) refers to it, was the 'most modern' place where this new world developed. Although its original growth was by streetcar suburbs like other US cities, by the 1920s Los Angeles already had more automobiles per capita than anywhere else in the world. In addition, as the fastest-growing American city in the first decades of the twentieth century, Los Angeles realtors and developers were especially powerful in local politics. The result was the 1926 approval of a massive bond issue to fund a large road network to overcome development constraints (Fishman, 1987, p. 166). Los Angeles became the city of the automobile, the city that could spread out across the landscape for mile after mile. As a city of suburbs, differentiation was achieved through concentrating more expensive homes on hills looking down on cheaper suburbs: Hollywood stars lived in their mansions in Beverly Hills. But the idea was still suburbia for all.

With the building of urban freeways across all American major cities in the early post-World War II years, suburbia becomes the dominant settlement form in the USA. At the other end of the social spectrum from Beverly Hills came the 'Levittowns' of the North East which brought suburban living to almost anybody with a regular job. The Levitt building company specialized in the modern mass production of suburbs. Peter Hall (1988, p. 295) describes their methods as based upon 'flow production, division of labour, standardised designs and parts, new materials and tools, maximum use of prefabricated components, easy credit, good marketing'. The latter facilitated mass consumption; people queued for hours to buy their piece of suburbia. In his survey of 'Levittowners', Herbert Gans (1967, p. 37) finds that the reason people gave for moving to this suburbia was that 'they wanted the good and comfortable life for themselves and their family'. In terms of aspirations, Gans (p. 39) identifies two that stand out: 'comfort and roominess' and 'privacy and freedom of action'. These are quintessentially concepts of ordinary modernity. Living in suburbs enabled manual workers to identify themselves as middle class (Halle, 1984): in suburbia the middle class became the universal class.

Initially the suburban route to middle-class comfort was not itself universal. Fishman (1987, chapter 4) describes it as an Anglo-American phenomenon in the nineteenth century, with the middle classes in the rest of Europe and the Americas staying much more loyal to traditional urban residential preferences. But with American hegemony and consequent Americanization, the middle class suburb has spread to cities across the world. The particular form that suburbs take varies between countries but the ideal of suburbia as collective comfort remains: people who can afford it move to suburbs for a better family life. Throughout the world, 'however modest each suburban house might be, suburbia represents a collective assertion of class wealth and privilege' (Fishman, 1987, p. 4). This landscape of consumer modernity represents the culmination of four centuries of ordinary modernity, it is a true monument of the modern world, the modern equivalent to the great Gothic cathedrals of the high middle ages in feudal Europe.

Not modernism

Before I leave the topic of ordinary modernity I need to make a short digression on modern architecture. Although suburbia has won the hearts and minds of ordinary people in the twentieth century, this has not extended to the professionals who deal with such matters. Architects and planners have conducted what Peter Hall (1988, p. 297) calls the 'great debate' on suburbia, but in a very one-sided manner. Professionals have consistently condemned the twentieth-century American city as representing the death of civilized urbanism: Hall refers to this as the 'architects' revenge', devising very negative metaphors such as 'octopus', 'lice along a tape worm' and 'disfiguring disease' to describe 'urban sprawl'. No wonder Herbert Gans (1967, p. v) has referred to suburbia as 'a much maligned part of America'.

I will interpret this difference between popular and professional evaluations of suburbia as reflecting a profession burdened by association with a dying modernity. Part of the problem of modern architecture is that it has been unable to accommodate to a modernization of modernity. This is largely because, as part of the modernism movement, modern architects believed they were themselves at the cutting edge of urban change. However, the truth is that modernist architecture and planning have been imbued with an ideology of industrialization. When a leading modern architect describes a house as 'a machine to live in', he lets the cat out of the bag: his ideas can be identified immediately as belonging to a stable of ideas which derive from Britain's industrial modernity. Hence popular suburbia and modern architecture have represented two very different paths to modernity, one a legacy of nineteenth-century modernity, the other the locus of twentieth-century modernity. It is hardly surprising, therefore, that they are not only different, in many respects they are the opposite of each other.

This opposition can be illustrated by the ideas of Le Corbusier, the doyen of modern architecture. He thought the design of cities 'was too important to be left to citizens' and was a great admirer of authoritarian leaders because they had the power to raze existing cities to the ground and start anew. So much for ordinary people and their concerns! There could hardly be a greater contrast with what Rybczynski (1986, p. 220) calls the 'democratization of comfort' experienced during the twentieth century. Hence comfort was the very least of Le Corbusier's concerns: in one famous case, the student accommodation he designed for the University of Paris had windows designed not to open – with the obvious corollary: nobody would live in them during the summer (Harvey, 1989, p. 36). His most famous building is the Unité d'Habitation on the outskirts of Marseilles which has been described in one book on modern architecture as 'probably the most significant [building] in post-war Europe' (Richards, 1962, p. 107). However, it was not intended to be a place in which to create homes: this 'compact, slab-like building, raised on tapering concrete columns, housing 1,600 people' was designed according to the criteria of minimum efficiencies, resulting in very small apartments (Richards, 1962, p. 152). Their size was made possible because there were communal services for typical family activities like child care, cooking and cleaning. For instance, instead of a personally cooked meal eaten in the family dining room, residents of the Unité were expected to eat in a cafeteria on the roof (Hall, 1988, p. 210). It is difficult to imagine anything more unlike suburbia. Of course, the residents themselves did not share the architect's modernism and decorated the building in the style of suburban France, cramming their flats 'with plastic chandeliers, imitation Louis XIV *bergères*, and Monoprix ormolu – just the furniture Corbusier struggled against all his life' (Hughes, 1991, p. 190). Although an extreme example, Le Corbusier has been very influential – witness unpopular public high-rise residential development in post-World War II Europe – and is by no means exceptional as a representative of the art world's modernism.

Whatever the debates going on in the high cultural realms of modern architecture, the suburban ideal won the battle of ideas because of, in Fishman's (1987, p. ix) words, 'enough support from ordinary people in the real world to transform the structure of the modern city'. This power, derived from 'the compelling vision of the modern family', has relegated professional architecture and planning to a minor, largely malign, role in the story of twentieth century residential development (1987, p. x). As a generic modernity some four hundred years in the making, ordinary modernity transcends such 'styles' as modernism and ultimately will dismiss those incompatible with its core character: by neglecting comfort, modern architecture was condemned, ultimately, to irrelevance.

4

Modern States

With the end of the Cold War, the democratic practice of electing governments has spread to more and more countries. Always an important ideological tool of the USA in its conflict with the USSR, today more than ever modern politics is democratic politics. It has not always been thus; contemporary liberal democracy can be interpreted as the political form of state emanating from American hegemony. This contrasts with the merchant oligarchic politics of the hegemonic Dutch and the liberal constitutionalism of the hegemonic British (Taylor, 1996a, chapter 2). But in all three states new participations in politics were consonant with the existence of an evolving ordinary modernity. Culminating in state-based representative democracy, for all its practical faults and political biases, widespread universal suffrage means that ordinary men and women have a direct input into government-making.

One way in which political elites have protected their power from democratic intrusion has been to invent a distinction between 'high' and 'low' politics. The latter is what democratic politics is all about, economic and social policies which impinge directly on the lives of ordinary people. High politics derives historically from the military and foreign policy reserved for the monarch and his militarily inclined aristocratic supporters. In contemporary politics it is concerned with the nature and position of the state in the wider world.

In this way foreign and defence policies have been much less prone to democratic influence than domestic policies. In the USA, for instance, the convention is for party politics to end at the shoreline, meaning that American politicians do not criticize American policy abroad. Another sign of this separation in politics is the fact that the British Foreign Office is by far the most independent of government departments. Generally, state-based representative democracy has had a profound impact on domestic policies but much less so on foreign policies. In practice, peace movements and anti-nuclear movements which oppose government policy can easily be portrayed as being against the state itself: in other words, they are tarred with the label traitor.

It is very interesting that this dual structure of modern politics is embedded in how the modern state is studied. There are two largely distinct bodies of literature, one dealing with the state as a political entity and another treating relations between states. This division of effort is institutionalized, in terms of university departments, learned societies and journals, as the disciplines of 'political science' and 'international relations' respectively. I can think of no other subject matter where a distinction between the one and the many constitutes an intellectual boundary. It seems to me that any credible understanding of modern states requires not only to overcome this odd division by recombining the two elements but also to investigate how the division came about in the first place and what it tells us about modern politics.

Political science is, with sociology and economics, one of the three primary social sciences and as such is much more sophisticated in its treatment of states than international relations. Focused upon the theory of the state, there has been a long-standing debate between various schools of Marxism and between them and non-Marxists. The problem with this work is that it is what it says it is, a theory of the state in the singular. Stripped to its bare essentials, it consists of different ways of understanding how a state relates to its civil society. While this relation is of fundamental importance, this is no excuse for neglecting the fact that in the modern world there is a multiplicity of states which obviously impinge upon one another. Viewed from this perspective, even the most sophisticated 'theory of the state' reads like a meaningless abstraction, a theory of the isolated state. One effect of this has been the relative neglect of war in this literature: Michael Mann (1988, p. viii) calls social science 'absurdly pacific' in its interpretation of states.

International relations has been more practitioner-orientated in its work, often seeing itself as an aid to 'statecraft'. In its dominant 'realist' form, it justifies its separate disciplinary existence on the grounds that relations between states are governed by anarchic conditions in which simple power relations rule. Beyond social rules, and therefore conventional social science, realist international relations assesses the dangers of the contemporary inter-state power configurations. As the obverse of political science treatments of states, realists ignore the internal nature of states, treating them as 'black boxes' – in one quite apt analogy, as billiard balls careering into one another. It is an argument for perennial war-preparedness; international relations has been widely criticized for being 'absurdly militant' in its interpretation of states.

In terms of modernity there is a further fundamental difference in these two studies of states. In realist international relations there is no recognition of the existence of distinctively 'modern' states; all states are viewed as being inherently war-like whether in the class-ical world, in the modern world, or any other world. In contrast, political science is more historically sensitive and typologies of dif-ferent categories of state exist: despotic, feudal, etc. In this approach theories of the state treat the modern state as distinctively capitalist or liberal depending upon the particular theory. This means that there are reasonable understandings of modern 'stateness' but only a sketchy sense for modern 'inter-stateness'. This is abundantly clear from the very term international relations: it is not what it says – about relations between 'nations' – its subject matter is inter-state relations. Stateless nations such as Flemings, Kurds and Zulus are not prime actors in international (sic) relations but multinational states such as Belgium, Turkey and South Africa are. To avoid such confusion I use the term inter-stateness to cover much that is implied by the concept of international relations. I define inter-stateness as both the practical mutuality and recognition that underlies modern states' relations with one another, and the modern way of thinking which sees the world as a multiplicity of states, as the political mosaic represented by the world political map. If, as G. Poggi (1978, p. 13) argues, it is 'the very nature of the modern state that there should be many states', this is where to begin.

Inter-stateness

The key conceptual development in the creation of modern politics was the conversion of the concept of sovereignty from a universal to a multiple condition. In Roman law, and in world-empires generally, sovereign power is vested solely in the emperor as lord of the world: *dominus mundi*. Hence the modern practice of identifying several 'empires' within a single political system in the wake of European colonial expansion is illogical from the perspective of the original imperial concept. For instance, historians invariably refer to the result of sixteenth-century Spanish conquests in the Americas as 'the Spanish Empire' but this is not how contemporaries viewed it (Elliot, 1989, p. 7). In their world there was only one empire, the Holy Roman Empire; their new conquests could not constitute a second or rival sovereignty. When the Spanish king was elected Holy Roman Emperor in 1519 as Charles V his imperial title had nothing to do with his overseas 'empire' and everything to do with the power of his family, the Habsburgs, in central Europe. However, this dynastic combination of Spanish territories with the Holy Roman Empire did revive ideas of universal monarchy just as the modern world-system was coming into being (Yates, 1975). As Tilly (1975) has emphasized, there was nothing inevitable about the rise of inter-stateness and Charles V as the 'second Charlemagne' briefly seemed to offer the possibility of an imperial peace for what were becoming politically stressful times.

The major advantage the imperial idea had in this age of transition was that it was the only form of political stability that was historically known and could therefore be envisaged. The Roman Empire represented the great golden age of peace and its legacy was periodically claimed to denote a new age of universal stability, notably with the Carolingian Empire after the crowning of Charlemagne by the Pope in 800. Charles V as Holy Roman Emperor claimed direct historical lineage from Charlemagne but the medieval origins of his imperial power limited the practical possibilities of a new political universalism. The Holy Roman Empire had always shared its sovereign status with the Papacy through a dual division of authority over the secular and spiritual respectively. This accommodation finally broke down in the twelfth century with the political defeat of the Empire by the Papacy (Strayer, 1970, p. 22). But without the temporal power to replace the Empire by a theocracy, political opportunity was created for other polities to construct their own political autonomies. City-states in Italy and medium-sized states in the rest of Western Europe outside Germany (the continuing core of the weakened Empire) took advantage of this situation. This was the world inhabited by Charles V as the last Emperor for whom universal pretensions were a practical possibility, however slight.

The 'victory' of the medium-sized states in the sixteenth and seventeenth centuries eliminated both Empire and Italian city-states as major players in the emerging modern world-system. This was a long historical process which can be dated from 1494 – the invasion of city-state Italy by France and then Spain – to the Treaty of Westphalia in 1648: the final abolition of the universal claims of both Empire and Papacy. The reasons why medium-sized states seemed to have survival advantages in the early modern period are to do with mobilization of resources for war. But this of itself does not explain the creation of modern inter-stateness as routine political relations between states.

In his exploration of the medieval origins of the modern state Strayer (1970, p. 27) points out that it is stateness rather than inter-stateness which was developed first. Early processes of state centralization involved only institutional development for 'domestic' affairs because 'in a Europe without states and without boundaries the concept of foreign affairs had no meaning.' Furthermore, with the full emergence of states in the sixteenth century it was not inevitable that politics would be organized around a distinction between 'domestic' and 'foreign' policies. For instance, David Sylvan (1987) provides a typology of different ways in which politics can be organized based in part on whether foreign affairs exist. On his criteria, the Renaissance city-states of Italy did not have foreign policies – relations between cities were not considered to be a separate category of politics because politicians recognized no distinction between domestic and foreign. In general, according to Charles Tilly (1985, p. 518), in the sixteenth and seventeenth centuries the distinction between domestic and foreign policies remained 'blurred'. Strayer (1970, p. 83) explains the situation thus: 'The concept of "foreign affairs" could hardly exist in a Europe that admitted the fact that it was made up of congeries of sovereign states but was not quite sure what states were sovereign.'

Clarification of who was and who was not sovereign is an underestimated achievement of the Treaty of Westphalia. Although properly considered to be the founding statement of the modern inter-state system, this is attributed mainly to acceptance of the principle of non-interference in one another's internal affairs, which is dealt with in the next section. While this is important as the first international law, there is the prior requirement to ascertain who receives such protection. At Westphalia the roll call of members of the inter-state system was agreed: the Dutch Republic and Switzerland were finally recognized as independent and in Germany political units were consolidated from 900 to 300 (Gross, 1968). From this time forth sovereignty has been recognized as a mutual recognition of states by states. Without this mutuality there is no inter-stateness. Hence formal inter-stateness and the final defeat of pre-modern universalism can be dated from Westphalia. No wonder Pope Innocent X was to condemn the treaty famously as 'null, void, invalid, unjust, damnable, reprobate, inane, empty of meaning and effect for all time' (Holsti, 1991, p. 25)!

It is this notion of political division based on sovereignty devised in seventeenth-century Europe that is the basis of today's comprehensive inter-stateness. For instance, in the decolonization after World War II, independent states confirmed their newly won status by joining the United Nations – the (near) universal club of states. James (1984, p. 2) defines sovereignty as 'the ground rule' of inter-state relations in that it identifies the territorial entities who are eligible to participate in the game of 'international relations'. The essence of sovereignty is that it provides 'international capacity' through mutual recognition. For instance, the Turkish Republic of Northern Cyprus set up after the invasion of Cyprus by the Turkish army in 1974 is recognized only by its creator Turkey. It has no international capacity. Similarly, the 'Bantustans' created by apartheid South Africa as 'independent black homelands' were not recognized as independent except by their creator and hence were never sovereign. What this means is that sovereignty cannot be obtained by self-declaration. Effective control of a territory – 'internal sovereignty' – is only a condition used in appeals to the 'international community' for recognition. It is 'external sovereignty' that finally counts.

Thus far inter-stateness has been considered as a basic property of the modern world-system but that does not mean it has been unchanging. Three stages in the development of the modern inter-state system have been identified and relate to the three hegemonic states. The Treaty of Westphalia of 1648 is the defining international treaty of Dutch hegemony. It produced what Gross (1968, p. 65) has termed the era of the 'liberty of states' in which predatory behaviour was the norm in a manner not too unlike the realist depiction of international relations. Nevertheless an inter-stateness was created through the emergence of international law in which no universalist pretensions were countenanced. This was Voltaire's 'commonwealth divided into several states' and Burke's 'diplomatic republic of Europe' (Bull and Watson, 1984, p. 1). The Treaty of Vienna of 1815 is the defining international treaty of British hegemony. This created a stronger inter-stateness in what Hinsley (1982) calls 'the modern international system'. The 'liberty of states' was curtailed by the Concert of Europe through which the great powers attempted to control political change. This conservative geopolitics legitimated an informal hierarchy of states but multiplicity and mutuality remained cornerstones of the politics. The agreement setting up the United Nations at San Francisco in 1944 is the defining international treaty of US hegemony. According to Coplin (1968, p. 31) this marked a 'profound and historic shift' through the international outlawing of military aggression as a condition of United Nations membership. This is reflected, for instance, in the mid-century change of names for the state apparatuses which deal with external military matters from War Ministries (or Departments) to Defence Ministries (or Departments). The practical effect of this has been that political boundaries are effectively frozen. Contemporary Africa has provided insights here. There have been several cases in the recent past where states have become ungoverned as a result of civil war, Somalia and Liberia being classic examples. However, members of this new category of state-without-a-government have maintained membership of the United Nations, that is, they retain external sovereignty. Hence, unlike eighteenth-century Europe when there were outside predator states ready to partition weakly controlled sovereign territory, today sovereignty is preserved through a very powerful inter-stateness.

Of course, the mutuality of external sovereignty cannot be separated from internal sovereignty in modern politics. Sovereignty comes as a single package, which is why the United Nations has not been successful in eliminating warfare: most wars are now civil wars, with inter-state wars being very much the exception. But civil wars are precisely an activity 'protected' by internal sovereignty with outside states reluctant to intervene without the agreement of all parties to the war. Where one-sided intervention in civil wars does occur, either it is justified as defence of the recognized government (e.g. the USA in South Vietnam, the USSR in Afghanistan) or the support has to be clandestine (e.g. the USA in Nicaragua). Inter-stateness is enabling of a very dangerous modern politics.

Absolutism as a political way of life

Modern politics is a politics of absolute spaces. This very stark and simple organization of power is legitimated through treating state sovereignty as the fundamental building block, defining the legal personages, of international law. Not interfering in the internal affairs of a sovereign state means that modern politics is premised upon boundaries that have allowed individual states a free hand to terrorize their populations with little fear of external legal retribution. This is a blight of territorial absolutism at the heart of modern politics.

Territorial absolutism is unique to the modern world. As a political construction it makes up the other side of the story from which inter-stateness emerged. The crisis of feudalism was a crisis simultaneously for the economic, political and cultural reproduction of this particular pre-modern world-system. The rise of trading cities and the development of new centralized state apparatuses contributed greatly to overcoming the first two elements of the crisis, the economic and political, but in the cultural sphere the demise of the feudal order culminated in a deep fracture of Christendom. The Reformation and Counter-Reformation disrupted early modern Europe and led to the 'crisis of the seventeenth century'. The solution was territoriality. In the attempt to create order out of the religious turmoil of the period, the principle of *cujus regio e jus religio* was invented which committed the population of a territory to the creed of their prince. This was first evoked at the Peace of Augsburg in 1555 to cope with the spread of Protestantism in the Holy Roman Empire and became consolidated throughout Europe at the Treaty of Westphalia in 1648. The result was that the traditional universalism of Catholic Christendom was transformed into a Europe of absolute religious territories. For people who did not share their prince's faith, choices were stark: 'voice' was dangerous and to be avoided, leaving either 'loyalty' through religious conversion or 'exit' as religious refugee.

The subsequent transformation of early modern states into nation-states did not challenge territorial absolutism; rather, it gave it a new and even more politically divisive basis. As Mike Billig (1995, p. 130) argues: 'The world of nation-states, being constructed in the modernist mood, is a world of boundaries.' Religious schismatics were replaced by enemies of the people or 'national traitors' and would share the same fate as heretics. Religious conversions were replaced by national minority assimilations where languages rather than sacraments were eliminated. And instead of 'religious cleansing', refugees have become victims of ethnic cleansing as the means for generating homogeneous cultural spaces. The basis of politics might change, but in the modern world political territories continue regardless. In fact, it can be argued that the political absolutism of early modern Europe has survived in just one respect, territoriality.

The claim to uniqueness for territorial absolutism is important. Before and beyond early modern Europe there were many examples of competitive state systems, with warfare resulting in the winning and losing of territory. But nowhere was the concept of territorial sovereignty devised except in early modern Europe. Noninterference in the religious affairs of neighbouring states as agreed at Augsburg presumes acceptance of domestic integrity or internal sovereignty. For Rosenberg (1990, p. 254) 'Recognising the historical novelty of this circumstance is crucial': the modern state-form is the only one to have 'achieved or claimed, both an institutional and a practical, territorially ordered, monopoly of violence' (p. 258). The political implications of this are profound but often overlooked. Nation-states have become part of the modern world's taken-for-granted existence: embedded states represent absolutism as a political way of life.

The territorial blight at the heart of modern politics carries through to the late twentieth century. Containment of war is commonly invoked as a fundamental reason for the initial rise of the territorial state (e.g. Gottmann, 1973; Herz, 1976) but there is a price to pay for bounding coercion which may by now have outweighed its advantages. In modern warfare, those people unlucky enough to be inside the bounds of conflict are effectively abandoned. Bounding state violence facilitates human rights abuses as far as and including genocide, as the tragedy of Rwanda has recently reminded the world. And in such situations the modern call for a 'democratic solution' rings very hollow. And not just because of the terrible violence: in the modern world, democracy is also bounded. With 'national elections' at the heart of the claim to be 'democratic', the practice of democracy is territorial. But democracy presupposes a 'demos' or people whereas in most states across the world definitions of peoples are what is being increasingly contested. As Walzer (1992, p. 164) points out, you cannot have democracy with more than one 'demos'. With a multicultural electorate, elections are reduced to little more than ethnic headcounts to legitimate the majority group's majority. Hence, for instance, the Serbian boycott of the first democratic referendum in Bosnia and Irish nationalist reluctance to agree a Northern Ireland referendum as a vehicle for peace. In both cases boundaries separate these two nationalist communities from their 'people' and they would be very willing participants in an election in a wider (former-Yugoslavia, all-Ireland) territorial frame where they constitute the largest group. But that is the point: bounding democracies – narrow or wide – in such multi-ethnic situations defines the result before a vote is cast.

It is commonplace in contemporary politics to contrast democracy as a peaceful practice with political violence. People who pursue the latter politics are often portrayed as anti-democratic, unwilling to heed the verdict of the people as given through the ballot box. This type of argument betrays an embedded territorialism in which boundaries are not problematized as the means to define a 'demos'. In this way territorial absolutism prevents modern politics reaching its own democratic ideal.

Going Dutch

Modern states are more than territorial monopolies of violence (or democracy), of course. Territorialism may have been the solution to early modern religious conflict, and had a national make-over later on, but this story misses out the critical economic role of modern states. And this is where the hegemons are important to modern state development; they produced new contents for political territories. As the first hegemons, the Dutch are particularly important in this respect.

The modern concept of the 'state' as a fundamental legal concept originates in the sixteenth century in France (Skinner, 1978; Dyson, 1980). In many ways France was with the most 'modern' form of state in the seventeenth century especially with its functional divisions of the state apparatus as a bureaucracy. The key point, however, is that, looking beyond institutions to state practices, it is the United Provinces that appear pre-eminently as the precursor of modern states. Boogman (1978) has made this argument most explicitly in terms of an emerging *raison d'état* that paralleled the rise of new political institutions.

The term *raison d'état* originally emerged as part of the process whereby the politics of states were separated from more general religious imperatives. Controversial and even sinful, the concept defined a necessary step in the creation of modern politics. It developed in the seventeenth century to make the interests of the state, usually the monarch, the pre-eminent political purpose. When attached to 'the glory of the king', *raison d'état* became generally associated with the 'aggressive expansion-seeking military-power state' (Boogman, 1978, p. 58). It is in this context that the Dutch Republic was so unusual. Boogman (1978, p. 60) refers to the new state's 'utter distaste for territorial expansion' – there was even a tendency for 'territorial contraction'! For instance, this was the position of the political school associated with Spinoza (Kossmann, 1963, p. 15) and can be found in the work of Peter de la Court – 'hedge-hog like contraction' (Kossmann, 1963, p. 16) – and Aitzema: 'This state has enough fortresses and land, even perhaps too many' (Rowen, 1978, p. 253).

This does not mean, of course, that the United Provinces had no *raison d'état* as Braudel (1984, pp. 205–6) has implied. Rather, the new state evolved its own particular 'economic' brand of state interest, which I suggest is more important historically than the usual geopolitical one. Boogman argues that the latter has been greatly overemphasized in early modern political histories at the expense of the Dutch invention. The two variants of *raison d'état* he terms 'continental-monarchical' and 'maritime-republican'. In the latter, economic interests came before political-military interests in defining state policy. In short, the state was regarded as a function of society not vice versa. Instead of society being viewed as a source of taxes and soldiers to expand the state through territorial accumulation, the state becomes a source of power to expand society through capital accumulation. At other times and places such ideas appeared as the 'Manchester School' of political economy and as President Calvin Coolidge's famous dictum that 'the business of America is business'. The point is that the regents of the Dutch 'merchant state' invented this ultra-modern state form in the seventeenth century.

For the Dutch the result was a unique new form of state where economic and political power seemed to merge. For instance, according to Klein (1982, p. 87) 'Dutch foreign policy was an undisguised assistance to trade.' The most quoted example is the intervention of the Dutch fleet in the Baltic in the first half of the seventeenth century to impose what has been termed a *pax Neerlandia* to protect the 'mother trade'. Similarly, in the major new institutions of the period such as the VOC (East India Company), it is impossible to separate the political from the economic aspects; rather, it is 'an arm of the state', 'a unique politico-commercial institution' (Israel, 1982, pp. 70–1). A similar statement can be made about the new Bank of Amsterdam. Israel (1982, p. 435) sums up the situation succinctly: 'Politics and economics merged at every point.' This was well understood by contemporaries; one English petition to Cromwell's government complained: 'It is no wonder that these Dutchmen should thrive before us. Their statesmen are all merchants' (t'Hart, 1989, p. 679).

This invention of a new state form is of importance for more than adding economics to the political agenda of modern states. By stimulating mercantilism as territorial economic competition, the Dutch laid the basis for the survival of the modern world-system.

Historically, proto-capitalist world economies are relatively common but none of them was able to develop into a sustained capital-expanding system in the way the modern world-system did. These earlier economic networks were built upon transactions between cities but the latter proved to be no military match for aggressive territorial-expanding states. In contrast, the Dutch Republic combined the economic success of past city-states with the defensive capabilities of contemporary territorial states: it was a defensive league of cities with its own protective shell (Taylor, 1993b).

From the perspective of most of its participants, the hugely destructive Thirty Years War in the first half of the seventeenth century was more typical of a social system in decline than one which is generating a new world-system. The usual outcome to such political turmoil, as shown in other times and places, is a political-military victory by one of the warring factions or an outside force to create a new 'universal' world-empire, the very nemesis of modern politics. Certainly, Europe in its 'crisis of the seventeenth century' looked ripe for a traditional centralization by military means, if not by the Habsburgs then subsequently by France. But the Dutch, with their 'golden age', showed an alternative route out of the turmoil. By making money respectable in their haven of peace and thereby enabling ordinary people to become subjects rather than objects of history, the Dutch hit upon a political formula for a new world that could defeat traditional power politics. They invented what might be called a 'bourgeois virtuous circle', a modern political economy to successfully resist traditional political military imperatives.

There is, thus, a sense in which today's modern world-system is the Dutch Republic writ large. As state exchequers moved from being taxation agencies and military procurers to becoming economic facilitators recognizably modern states come into view. By the end of the nineteenth century close relations between government, industry and banks were widely accepted in what was to be called state monopoly capitalism. The renewed bout of state economic competition at this time is sometimes known as the 'new mercantilism'. In the twentieth century this state–business alliance is usually referred to as 'corporatism' and may include labour in the devising of state economic policy. But it has been since the two decades after World War II, American high hegemony, that economic growth has become the key criterion for assessing state success. Per capita GNP league tables have become common fare as all states become 'development states' whose prime functions are to promote economic growth within their respective territories. Nobody today should doubt the importance of the original Dutch *raison d'état*.

The changing nature of territoriality

The modern political practice of territoriality has extended beyond the realms of defence and mercantilism, of course. As a politics which controls entry and exit it has the potential to change and mould the contents and therefore the nature of a territory. This potential has been exploited in modern politics to create ever-changing forms of state. Thus the combination of defence and political economy that the Dutch pioneered is a starting point for increasingly complex political development beyond the original political economy. Modern states have evolved with the modern world to become uniquely large political institutions with vast ranges of functions most of which could never have been contemplated in pre-modern states.

The key change has been the territorial containment of culture to create the concept of nation-state. Early modern states were created by a mixture of dynastic legacy, conquest and alliance wherein any actual political affiliation to the state was limited to a small political class with little or no penetration to ordinary people. However, the power of modern states is based to a large degree upon the fusing of the idea of state with that of nation to produce nation-states. This power has been created by the fundamental territorial link that exists between the concepts of state and nation. All social institutions exist concretely in some section of space but state and nation are both peculiar in having a special relation with a specific place. Just as a given state has sovereign power in a particular territory, a nation has meaning only in relation to a particular place, its homeland. It is this basic communality of state and nation as both being constituted through their locations that has enabled them to be linked together as nation-state (Taylor, 1993a).

The entry of the 'people' on to the political stage as 'nation' was facilitated by the Enlightenment and the 'discovery' of progress. As noted in chapter 2, the Dutch prospered before economic development was interpreted as progress – the original mercantilist theories posited a static world – but in the eighteenth century the idea of economic 'improvement' was just one aspect of a general confrontation with all traditional social relations culminating in the French Revolution. Progress came to be viewed not just as possible but as being the norm. This modern intellectual accommodation to incessant change had the effect of discrediting not just static mercantilism but the whole traditional edifice of society. It was in these circumstances that ordinary people who had been mere objects of change entered history as subjects of change, laying the basis of a new national politics.

When the new rationality focused upon the sovereignty basis of states, the 'people' were discovered as the true source of legitimation, replacing the sovereign and his discredited religious claims to authority. In the American Revolution the people were interpreted as consisting of the commercial classes but with the French Revolution the full radical implications of the change in sovereignty were revealed (Billington, 1980). The people became the nation, all citizens of the state. Furthermore, as a nation the people were deemed to share crucial cultural attributes so that their citizenship was not an arbitrary matter of location. The nation was, in Benedict Anderson's (1983) famous phrase, an imagined community. It became a collective group with a common destiny. In this way national identity replaced religious identity as the basis for incorporating individuals into the political arena. In addition, the community was indissolubly linked to the land in which it developed. This completely changed the nature of territory, especially the integrity of its borders. From being parcels of land transferable between states as the outcome of wars, all territory, including borderlands, became inviolate. This changing meaning of territory can be seen in the 1793 French Constitution which debarred government from ever making peace with a foreign power that occupied any part of French territory (Billington, 1980, p. 66). In short it became the state's duty to defend the national homeland.

The national homeland became a cultural container. And herein lies the secret of how nationalism helped ordinary men and women to cope with the social upheavals they experienced. It is no accident that the rise of nationalism coincided with the great nineteenth-century economic restructurings of industrialization and consequent urbanization (Nairn, 1981). The land was being made sacred just as vast numbers of the people were being forced to leave it and move to towns and cities. National culture gave people a continued identity with their land. As its landscape became imbued with historical significance, the community of people who had once lived there, sharing the same language, were given a glorious, if sometimes tragic, shared past which pointed the way to their future common destiny.

In the first half of the nineteenth century nationalism continued in the French tradition as a revolutionary movement at war with multinational dynastic states. This was transformed in the second half of the century with the emergence of 'official' nationalisms (Anderson, 1983). States discovered the efficacy of the new cultural container and nurtured it. Basically state managers found the idea of nation very conducive to mobilizing its citizens behind the state: from the sponsoring of national 'high culture' to feeding the people their national history in the schools and the much more sinister nationalizing programmes (policies such as Russification, Germanification, Anglification, etc.), states hitched their destinies to nationalism. Those that didn't disappeared with World War I.

In the twentieth century the nation-state has become ubiquitous. All states, however many different ethnic groups live in their territories, are assumed to be 'nation-states' or, worse, simply 'nations'. Conflating state and nation is endemic to modern language and is given legitimacy by the name given to the nearly universal states' institution, the United Nations (sic). Today the world consists of about 200 of these cultural containers (the numbers having recently risen) within which national ideals are being reproduced in schooling, the mass media and all manner of other social institutions. Much of this politics might be 'top-down' but the revolutionary potential of nationalism cannot be wholly eliminated. Whatever use is made of it, the idea of the people as a nation remains a profoundly democratic concept.

The basic question nationalism prompts is: if we are all part of the same community surely we should all have the same rights and obligations? This was explicit in the original French revolutionary nationalism where adult male suffrage and military conscription were soon implemented. When nationalism became widely adopted in Europe as official state doctrine a century later, the implications for the political process were soon to be found on each state agenda. Suffrage reform proceeded at different rates in different countries but no state avoided a massive increase in its political citizenry (Rokkan, 1969).

This had a profound effect on states and their operations. Mobilizing voters required policies targeted at the newly enfranchised citizens. In addition new parties – socialist, peasant, church – were taking advantage of the widened suffrage to compete with established parties using completely new programmes – these are dealt with in the next chapter. The result of all this was to bring the concerns of ordinary people on to the agendas of states. As right and left wing political elites competed for government a new set of functions was added to states' apparatuses. Whether the social imperialism of the right, the new liberalism of the centre or the social democracy of the left, all contributed to the development of social policies which came to be called the 'welfare state'. Although taking different forms in different countries, its essence was to treat the people of a state as a society, a cohesive social grouping that constituted a moral and practical social system. That is to say, states had a moral obligation to look after their peoples by providing a social safety net and a practical task of making sure societies functioned properly by preventing a breakdown of social order.

Modern states of the twentieth century have been the end result of all these processes. States have become the great container of activities, first capturing politics (defence), then economics (mercantilism), followed by cultural identity (nationalism) and finally the idea of society (welfare) itself. This fusing of polity, economy, nation and society has produced the most powerful of all institutions in the twentieth century, so powerful in fact that for much modern discourse 'the state' has masqueraded as a pseudo-natural phenomenon, a taken-for-granted abstraction rather than a multiple historical creation.

I have been careful throughout this chapter to refer to states rather than 'the state' in the singular. It is very difficult to keep an eye on inter-stateness when dealing with stateness but that is what is needed in working towards a theory of states. Even where states are recognized in their plurality, often the focus remains on the state in the singular. For instance, the widely used Open University text *States and Societies* (Held, 1984) begins, despite its title, by informing the reader that 'this book focuses on the modern state' (p. ix) before the editor introduces the readings with an essay entitled 'Central perspectives on the modern state'. From the perspective of this chapter, the singular cast of such language is more applicable to pre-modern worlds than the modern world-system. Rosenberg (1990, p. 258) uses a very pertinent simile to make this point: 'A modern state out of the state system is like a fish out of water; it literally cannot breathe; it cannot even secure its domestic sovereignty.' In other words, a theory of the state is a study of states as if they existed only like dead fish on a fishmonger's slab: their anatomy can be understood but not much about what they actually do. The geohistorical perspective of this chapter has tried to point the way beyond such surrealist theories of the state which have no concept of inter-stateness, and realist international (sic) relations which has no concept of modernity.

5
Political Movements

Hegemonic modernities do not go uncontested. Turning old worlds upside down provides opportunities for some but threatens and destroys the lives of others. The grievances produce a complex pattern of radical and reactionary actions to counter the social changes. The most obvious reaction is to devise means of stemming unwanted changes. From below this is the tradition of throwing a spanner in the works such as Luddite machine-smashing, from above there has been the equally long tradition of socially demeaning 'trade'. Thus far both have been to little avail as hegemonic modernities have swept all before them. A more subtle approach has been to accept the fact that a new world has been created and to devise alternative 'new worlds' with a preferred social structure. It is these purveyors of alternative worlds that are of concern here.

As previously noted, the early modern world in which the hegemonic Dutch operated was different from later modern periods in two vital respects. First, political conflict was still framed in religious terms and, second, there was no overriding theory of progress in the social consciousness. In this pre-Enlightenment period, cultural reaction to the new capitalist world-economy incorporated an enhanced geographical imagination (Clarke, 1979; Zerubavel, 1992). Bringing the Americas into Europe's orbit destroyed classical cosmology and stimulated both the factual study of new worlds in geography and the new fictional genre of utopias in which new worlds were invented. In the seventeenth century the Dutch as hegemons became the world information centre, specializing in cartography and all forms of travel writing (W. D. Smith, 1984; P. Allen, 1992). In this particular context of religion and geography without the cultural tools to imagine building a better world *in situ*, the ultimate solution to social grievances was for a 'chosen people' to find a 'promised land'. This 'exodus' political option contributed to the spread of European settlement across the world but was never a challenge to the system itself. By its very nature this creation of alternative new worlds attempted to avoid rather than resist the system. However, the strategy has continued in later eras, notably in Owenite socialism and its emulators in nineteenth-century community developments and in the contemporary commune movement stemming from the 1960s. But these have been relatively minor reactions to later modernities. With the development of a new historical imagination of progress in the eighteenth century, politically consolidated by the French Revolution, the idea of creating new worlds *in situ* became possible, leading to the emergence of new politics of resistance and change.

Building new worlds *in situ* requires political movements which challenge the system, anti-systemic movements in world-systems parlance. These are general political movements which attempt to mobilize populations to change the fundamental nature of the modern world. In this chapter I focus upon two such movements in particular, the socialist and the environmental. The reasons for this selection will become clear as I proceed. I begin by continuing the discussion of the last chapter. Modern politics is about states, to be sure, but what goes on within states is organized through political parties. In practice, therefore, most people experience modern politics as party politics. This equation was confirmed in modernization theory, wherein political development was seen as change towards a stable democratic politics of competitive political parties. But many political parties derive from radical movements; here I use a geohistorical interpretation of parties to link movements to modern politics as a prelude to relating them back to prime modernities.

Parties and movements

According to Neumann (1969, p. 26), political parties are the 'great intermediaries' of modern politics. In this crucial role they link 'social forces and ideologies to official government institutions and [relate] them to political action within the larger political community'. With the exception of a few traditional dynastic regimes (largely in the Middle East) and military dictatorships, political parties are found in states across all continents of the world. But parties are only a recent success: according to Duverger (1954) in 1850 only the USA had modern political parties. Traditional suspicion of parties has emanated from their role as 'part' of a polity: representing a division in the polity, they were seen as a potential source of conflict. The most famous such condemnation was by George Washington in his Farewell Address where he warned of the divisiveness of 'parties' for national unity. However, he did not mean parties in the modern sense but, rather, what are usually termed political factions. How such factions, endemic to all polities pre-modern and modern, evolved into modern parties is my concern here.

Generally a distinction can be drawn between factions serving special interests and parties organized by principles. The latter claim to represent the public interest but differ in their particular perspectives on what constitutes the public or national interest. Hence modern political parties have ideological labels such as liberal, conservative, democrat, socialist, republican, and so on. In Britain, for instance, in about 1850 the loose parliamentary groupings known as Whigs and Tories were transformed into the Liberal and Conservative parties respectively. Such parties are termed cadre parties because they remained vehicles for political elites in their parliamentary competition. Initially organized in Parliament, as the franchise was extended they needed to organize supporters in the country in order to compete in elections involving more and more voters. Such parties were very successful in the nineteenth century and between them kept control of government. Gradually they came to be challenged by a very different type of party whose origins were in the country rather than the parliament. Mass parties were 'bottom-up' organizations which attempted to mobilize newly enfranchised voters, usually direct producers – workers and peasants. New parties for mobilization, of both labour/socialist and agrarian/populist hues, emerged from existing political movements. Their power base was the opposite to the cadre parties: in mass parties, parliamentary or assembly members were viewed as party delegates, accountable to party members. By the beginning of the twentieth century both cadre and mass parties were to be found competing for government in most European states. It is these 'party systems' which, according to Rokkan (1969), became 'frozen' to constitute the modern pattern of party politics in Western European democracies throughout the twentieth century. It is also at this time that the US party system diverges from those in Europe: both Populist and Socialist Parties failed to mobilize sufficient numbers to constitute credible rivals for government, leaving the USA with two, relatively loosely organized, cadre parties, Republican and Democrat.

Although in hindsight we know that the parties competing in 1900 survived through the twentieth century this should not be used to extrapolate backwards a political stability which did not exist. Cadre and mass parties were uneasy bedfellows; the former represented business as usual to be endorsed by election, the latter used elections to build support to change the system. Under pressure from the mass parties, cadre parties gradually extended their efforts to appeal to the 'grass roots', creating national organizations in a process Duverger (1954) has called 'contagion from the left'. They were thus transformed into 'representation parties' – less ideological institutions, more representing public opinion instead of trying to lead it (Blondel, 1978). After 1945 the mass parties gradually shed their ideologies also to become representation parties: socialist parties became as likely as conservative parties to employ pollsters to discern public opinion and trim their policies accordingly. With the demise of the mobilizing zeal, with no longer any attempt to convert the voters ideologically, representation party systems have become the norm in the second half of the twentieth century in European and European-settler democracies. This 'domestication of the left', as Rokkan (1969) calls it, brought European party systems into line with American political practices. Here the conversion of the two cadre parties into representation parties had created a 'consumer politics' with party leaders marketed like soap powders as the techniques of advertising become the indispensable tools of contemporary politics. The advent of New Labour in Britain is the classic culmination of this process. Called by the reformers 'modernization', it is, of course, an acute Americanization with 'old Labour' denigrated as ideological and the party machinery redesigned to marginalize 'activists': party conferences are like old-style American party conventions, more for cheer-leaders than policy-makers. Policy depends now on non-party focus groups.

It is a long political route from radical movement with the goal to change society to representation party with the goal to reflect society. There have been three steps in the domestication of socialist parties, alternatively called adaptation to changing times or collaboration with the enemy, depending on one's politics. The first step is directly due to Karl Marx's decision in the late 1860s to steer the socialist movement towards national party organization. The First International (1862) was a grouping of radical trade unions and other political groupings but not parties. It collapsed under the pressure of the Marxist versus anarchist debate and when resurrected as the Second International (1889) was composed solely of socialist parties organized state by state. This organizational development was justified by Marx (1972) in his *Critique of the Gotha Programme* of 1876 as class struggle being national 'in form' but international 'in substance'. However, the proof of the pudding came in 1914 when national socialist parties across Europe took sides in World War I for their states and against one another. The second step resulted from the nature of the party organization. In 1915 Robert Michels (1949) propounded his 'iron law of oligarchy' which basically said that socialist parties created their own political elite separated from the masses, not unlike traditional cadre parties. It is at this point that the socialist movement bifurcated in reaction to the 1917 Russian Revolution. The third step for those parties which remained in the Second International was that their political elites eventually created representation parties in the context of the spread of affluence under American hegemony. In contrast, a revolutionary cadre party, the Bolsheviks, lead the way to a different ending. Those joining the Third International maintained an international socialist rhetoric throughout the Cold War but they disappeared as a radical force long before the political demise of the 'second world' in 1989–91.

Movements and modernities

The collapse of so-called 'real existing socialism' in Eastern Europe has been traumatic for the wider movement. According to André Gorz:

> As a system, socialism is dead. As a movement and an organized political force, it is on its last legs. All the goals it once proclaimed are out of date. The social forces which bore it along are disappearing. It has lost its prophetic dimension, its material base, its 'historical subject'. (Gorz, 1994, p. vii)

With the monumental demise of socialisms as anti-systemic movements in the late twentieth century, it is hardly surprising that radical hope for changing the world, for transforming the capitalist world-economy, has found a new focus in environmentalism.

In contrast to political debacle, the environmental movement seems to have gone from strength to strength. To be sure, the record of Green parties has been modest in national politics, but that is not where the real influence of this movement lies. In fact some activists have argued that 'a party is a counterproductive tool, . . . the given political space is a trap' (Bahro, 1986, pp. 210–11). Rather, environmentalists have been remarkably successful in two very different contexts: they have changed the way many people conduct their day-to-day lives and they have managed to place 'green' issues on to the agenda of world politics. No wonder John McCormick provides an upbeat assessment of the movement:

> Environmentalism has . . . spawned a mass movement with millions of followers, generated new bodies of law, hatched new political parties, encouraged a rethinking of economic and social priorities and become a central issue of international relations. For the first time, humanity has awakened to some of the basic truths about the interrelatedness of the biosphere. (McCormick, 1995, p. xi)

The global environmental movement has created a new universalism – saving life on Earth.

Of course, environmentalist writing is as susceptible to triumphalist tendencies as any other political discourse. One form this has taken has been a Whig interpretation of the history of environmentalism that searches for the 'roots' of the movement and traces progressive growth through to its contemporary importance. This use of history to celebrate the present and imply an inevitable future growth is an important ideological tool for all political movements. It certainly brings to mind early twentieth-century British political tracts charting the 'forward march of labour' and more generally the ideas of evolutionary socialism. However, by employing prime modernities as the framework for analysis, both socialism and environmentalism are given a geohistorical specificity in comparing them as anti-systemic movements. A key advantage of using this approach in this context is the way in which industrialization is treated. Both socialists and environmentalists have loosely employed a generalized 'industrialism' as the pervasive nature of modern society, usually without adequately appreciating the depth of changes in the system since the original 'industrial revolution'. This has allowed both environmentalists to project their movement Whiggishly back into the nineteenth century and socialists to project nineteenth-century conflicts forward through the twentieth century. By dividing this 'modern industrialism' into two distinct forms it is far easier to see the basic geohistorical relations between the two movements: socialism as prime resistance within industrial modernity and environmentalism as prime resistance to consumer modernity.

Unlike the Dutch, British hegemony operated in a world in which the idea of progress was naturalized: how else would societies change? Such a historical imagination had profound effects upon how social grievances could be politically marshalled. Edward Thompson's (1963) *The Making of the English Working Class* remains the classic historical text on this epochal change in the theory and practice of resistance. Opening up the future to political contest led to new tools of resistance: a political repertoire based upon spontaneity gradually gave way to new organized resistance with permanent institutions to prepare the path to a better future (Wallerstein, 1983, p. 61). It was in this context that socialism was invented as a reaction against the new industrial world which Britain was creating. The great political contradiction of British modernity was the rise of the proletariat resulting from the new production processes. And Marx's contribution was to set socialism within a historical process that linked past, present and future

(Schumpeter, 1942, p. 307; Fernbach, 1973). As such he was scathing in his criticism of utopian socialism: the exit option was no longer necessary now history could be harnessed to the cause. In combating industrialization, socialism was conforming to the basic parameters of nineteenth-century politics which were set by Britain's industrial revolution. Hence anti-systemic socialists and pro-systemic liberals, for about a century and a half, shared a common faith in world progress, albeit to different destinations, and belief in technology as a world force for liberation, albeit for different ends.

American hegemony was marked by the Cold War as the ultimate contest between capitalism and socialism culminating in the definitive defeat of the latter with the collapse of the USSR. This does not mean the end of anti-systemic movements, of course. The great political contradiction of American modernity is the depletion of the environment resulting from the new consumption processes. The very success of American capitalism has generated a very different reaction to the system in which both progress and technology are seen as problematic at best. A new 'post-modern' historical imagination is abroad that has replaced inevitable progress by a secular apocalypse if society continues unchanged. The idea that capitalism has reached or is reaching its limits in relation to the Earth has spawned the global environmental movement. Their organization has the goal of an alternative sustainable world but their immediate contemporary work is to prevent further environmental degradation. Hence national parties are less important than trans-state organization, environmental non-governmental organizations (NGOs), that combat environmental problems as global politics. Because socialist 'internationalism' was always stronger in rhetoric than in practice, this new organization has the potential for providing a system-wide effective opposition to capitalism for the first time.

Socialism against the modernity that Britain created

Britain's modernity was industrialization, the anti-systemic reaction to this was socialism: how does this simple proposition aid in interpreting the dramatic demise of socialism as a challenge to the capitalist world-economy? The fundamental answer is that the socialism built in the twentieth century was constructed out of a nineteenth-century modernity. In this sense the Communist Party of the USSR created a great 'nineteenth-century state' that ultimately found it impossible to survive within twentieth-century modernity. Thus it is entirely appropriate that the book (Goldman, 1972) which discovered Soviet industrial pollution of the environment had a nice nineteenth century ring to its title: *The Spoils of Progress*.

Socialism as an anti-systemic movement derives from, or is directly influenced by, the writings of Karl Marx. Working in London during British high hegemony, Marx was very clear about the particular modernity he was concerned with. In the preface to the original German edition of *Das Kapital*, Marx explained to his readers that he had chosen England 'as the chief illustration in the development of my theoretical ideas' because '[T]he country that is more developed industrially only shows to the less developed, the image of its own future' (Marx, 1954, p. 19). Here British industry defines modern society so that progress is equated with industrialization; it could be no other way given the time and place of the writer. But this image of modernity survived into the mid-twentieth century as socialist political practice. In updating Marxism, later theorists and politicians have focused upon European international developments in their theories of imperialism to the detriment of the contemporaneous domestic changes occurring in the USA. The main exception to this neglect is Gramsci's identification of 'Americanism' as 'a new beacon of civilisation' (Hoare and Smith, 1971, p. 316), but he was to have too little political influence on the development of socialism. Hence, while a new modernity was being created in America, Marxists were constructing an alternative society derived from the earlier British version of modernity. The result after 1945 was an Eastern European model of socialism consisting of a development strategy for industrialization with an emphasis on capital goods (Brucan, 1981, p. 100). Hence heavy industry – steel, coal, railways, engineering plus, of course, armaments – was promoted to build up productive and defence capacity while sacrificing consumer goods. In many ways the opposite of American affluent society, the USSR came to be denigrated as a 'third world country with rockets'.

The point is that the communist countries were pursuing an

economic strategy of 'catching up' but in relation to a modernity already superseded by Americanization. The initial successes of the strategy in terms of economic growth were therefore quite misleading. The building up of a heavy industrial base will obviously stimulate production but this alone can proceed only so far. From the first five-year plan in 1928 to 1978, Soviet industrial production increased 128 times (Brucan, 1981, p. 102). But this spectacular quantitative achievement was insufficient, what was lacking was qualitative change to a new modernity. As Gorz (1994, p. 10) has pointed out, such planning by pre-establishing targets can only 'consolidate existing structures'. More and more coal and steel was irrelevant in the context of a technology gap that inevitably resulted from emulating nineteenth-century industrialization. By the 1970s, growth rates were declining as the advantage of planning based upon a model of a 'known' industrial past was transformed into the disadvantages of planning in an uncertain present. Previously, extra investment had created additional growth but in the 1970s this relationship broke down leaving Soviet planning stranded in a past world (Brucan, 1981, p. 107). Quite simply, the severely inflexible accumulation of the East could not compete with the new flexible accumulation strategies evolving in the West.

Socialism as a political practice represented by the USSR therefore created its own cul de sac in the history of the modern world-system. Although based upon a genuinely anti-systemic movement from the nineteenth century, in the end it could not cope with the new modernity of the twentieth century. As an 'alternative world' the USSR was peddling a future that had less and less relevance to its own population and those of its allies as Americanization blossomed. The new consumption-based modernity vanquished all before it and took no prisoners. With the great benefit of hindsight, it is better now to refer to this defeated anti-systemic movement as *industrial* socialism. The addition of the adjective signifies a particular phase of opposition within the modern world-system that relates to Britain's industrial modernity. Its theories and practices focused upon the industrial working class, even in agrarian countries where workers constituted a very small proportion of the population. This included the USSR in 1917 and China in 1949, of course, plus all those post-colonial Marxist regimes where the idea of the proletariat as the vanguard of change was simply ludicrous.

Such a proletariat fetishism was finally exposed by the proletariat itself: industrial socialism was defeated when enough of the ordinary waged population – traditional working class and lower middle class – were won over by individualistic consumer society to undermine collectivist socialist models of social change.

Environmentalism against the modernity that America created

The above interpretation of socialism casts America winning the Cold War as something less than the triumph it was widely declared to be. For a variety of reasons and motives, the power of the USSR was fundamentally overestimated by friend and foe alike and with increasing benefit of hindsight its collapse is becoming less and less surprising. Today it can be seen that, despite the real threat of a nuclear war, the Cold War represented the final apogee of an anti-systemic challenge to a past modernity. The USA as the new modernity was overcoming the most resistant oppositional vestige of its predecessor.

The demise of industrial socialism more than a century after the end of British high hegemony defines a long politico-cultural time-lag. This reflects the reactive nature of the anti-systemic movement whose initial organization can be found in the final years of high hegemony – the First International was established by Marx in 1862 – but which only had a continuous international organization from 1889 with the Second International. A similar pattern can be seen in the rise of the environmental movement. Although there were many warnings about limits to growth in the 1940s and 1950s these were largely ignored in the wake of the social optimism generated by US-led world economic growth (McCormick, 1995, pp. 34–6). Environmentalism was transformed from minor lobby to mass movement in the wake of the success of Rachel Carson's exposé of the effect of insecticides in her *Silent Spring* in 1962. John McCormick (1995, chapter three) records the rapid rise in membership of environmental groups in what he calls the 'environmental revolution' of 1962–70 culminating in 'Earth Day' on 22 April 1970 in which some 300,000 people across the USA took part. This movement was consolidated internationally just as US high hegemony was waning with the UN conference on the environment at Stockholm in 1972, commonly seen as the pivotal event in the making of the global environmental movement (McCormick, 1995, p. 107).

The coincidences of *Silent Spring* appearing on the centenary of the First International and that, as opponents pointed out, Earth Day was also Lenin's birthday should not blind us to the very basic discontinuities between these new and old social movements. Just as Marx would have no truck with utopians, so environmentalists could not countenance socialist notions of industrial progress. Membership of environmental organizations was anything but proletarian: they were middle class in orientation, heavily biased towards new white-collar occupations. In the 1960s much environmental protest was naive and idealistic, making its radical credentials problematic at best. This meant that in the social turmoil of the decade, environmentalists were usually on the margins of major protest centred on particular issues such as civil rights and anti-war campaigns. The latter congealed into a generalized revolution in 1968 but this was the peak of the protest rather than a step towards practical social change. And it was environmental groups that benefited from the lost momentum of the other movements (McCormick, 1995, pp. 77–8). It was now that concern for environmental issues transcended lobbying tactics to cultivate a new politics based upon activism. This was symbolized by the establishment in 1969 of Friends of the Earth: demand for a more active campaign strategy within the Sierra Club was rebuffed, leading to this new overtly political, and soon to be international, environmental organization that was to typify the 1970s.

The *raison d'être* of all new social movements has been to create a new politics but it is the environmental movement more than any other that has promoted new organizations of opposition. Although non-governmental organizations (NGOs) predate the environmental revolution, their rapid recent growth coincides with the rise of the global environmental movement which has contributed disproportionally to the growth. Furthermore, environmental NGOs are generally much more independent of government than others; rather than being merely international, environmental NGOs are typically transnational and even global in nature. The emergence of these NGOs is, according to Princen and Finger (1994a, p. 10), indicative of a 'profound transformation' in world politics. This claim deserves serious consideration: are NGOs the equivalent organizational innovation to the party in the socialist movement?

Whereas the political party found its niche linking state and civil society in the development of national mass politics, Thomas Princen (1994) shows how environmental NGOs have carved out a political space for themselves between the government/intergovernment sector and the corporate sector in an evolving globalized politics. More than all other types of NGO, environmental ones are likely to be represented formally at international gatherings, not just for agenda setting but also within decision-making bodies. This is because of, first, the special scientific nature of the issues, which are outside the normal context of government and corporate expertise, and second, the legitimacy environmental NGOs have attained in representing neither narrow territorial nor market interests like the other world actors, states and corporations. In addition, environmental NGOs have a further distinctive role in bringing together the local and the global. By taking local issues and 'upstreaming' them – that is, moving the politics to higher levels in the global political hierarchy – environmental NGOs provide 'the alternative to delinking' through 'the construction of new linkages' (Princen, 1994, p. 40). In short, environmental NGOs have defined for themselves a crucial niche that other international actors are unable to fill. They may become the basis for the organizational innovation that the political party was for socialism.

It is probably too soon to assess adequately whether a critically new politics is in the making in the way suggested above. I have much sympathy with Steven Yearley's (1994, p. 160) position that the environmental movement has a 'better chance' of transcending national barriers than other putative global social movements. This is because the grievances this movement deals with transcend both state and market. Socialists probably came closest in the past to creating a system-wide organization of resistance but they were always merely international because they chose the basic political strategy of operating through national politics. In contrast, environmentalists deal with issues that are inherently trans-boundary in nature, such as pollution, and often fundamentally global, as with 'commons' such as the oceans or the ozone layer. This is not to refute the fact that in many third world countries NGOs work very closely with national governments; the point is that their politics is not intrinsically state-centric.

Of course, as with all movements, co-options into the system are to be expected: today's buoyant 'green consumer' business has parallels with Fabian socialist policies of 'permeation' at the turn of the nineteenth century. Leslie Sklair (1994) is right to remind us of such processes, but it is also the case that the 'deeper green' groups have developed an alternative world vision of an environmentally friendly society that transcends both state and capital. With a different value system, environmentalists emphasize the need to 'learn our way out of the crisis' so that the ultimate role of environmental NGOs could be as agents of social learning beyond state education and corporate research and development. Here their unusual, for a social movement, relation to scientific knowledge may be relevant. There is the prospect for the elimination of the state-embedded nature of social knowledge (Taylor, 1996b) and the reuniting of the 'two cultures' that separate science from the humanities (Princen, Finger and Manno, 1994; Wallerstein et al., 1996).

But there is one fundamental flaw in the global environmental movement as represented by NGOs: their democratic deficit. They are private organizations that guard their privacy closely (Princen and Finger, 1994a, p. 12). Although particular NGOs may have many members and even more numerous supporters, this is far removed from the structures of mass representation that socialist parties tried to construct in their heyday. This criticism is perhaps ironic given that Green parties in national politics have been the most innovative democratic instruments of recent times, but this practice has not been translated to politics beyond national arenas. In fact, it is hard to see how such 'party democracy' can be translated into NGO practice in international politics. Hence environmental NGOs have become influential and powerful without clear democratic accountability. How can they be made responsible and to whom? Is Greenpeace to be a perennial 'radical outsider' in local communities where environmental battles are fought? Socialists overcame their early era of 'outside agitators' through the development of the mass party that linked local concerns to national politics. Environmentalists have yet to create an equivalent innovative mechanism to show that their claim to link the local with the global can proceed in a meaningful participatory politics.

Overall, we can conclude that environmentalism, in reaction to America's consumer modernity, has created a genuinely anti-systemic movement but that its final democratic form has yet to be realized.

6

Geographical Tensions

The development theory which underlay the study of modernization in the 1950s and 1960s was based upon a geohistorical trick. The ruse consisted of substituting history for geography. Thus the contemporary differences between countries in terms of economic production were interpreted as different historical stages of a common historical trajectory: India was seen as being in the 'precondition to take off' stage in the 1960s and was fully expected to 'take off' after 1970, mimicking England's 'preconditions' of the 1740s leading to 'take off' after 1760. This social theory is about as simple as it can get: one multiple-repeated history, no geography. The latter is the case because irrespective of the location of a country in the world and its particular physical resources, the same temporal sequence of changes would befall it. Of course, this way of theorizing change has been widely criticized, as previously noted, but it is symptomatic of a wider malaise in social theory. As modernist projects, all the social sciences have had, as their prime purpose, to understand social change. As such they have devised historical imaginations and neglected geographical imagination (Soja, 1989). I have termed my study a geohistorical interpretation and that means I do not follow the tradition of overlooking space. In this chapter I focus on the 'geo'.

Fortunately, the neglect of the spatial has been widely addressed from a variety of perspectives. The starting point has often been the observation of Michel Foucault (1980, p. 70) that whereas time has been treated as dynamic, space is seen as essentially 'dead'. This observation has been taken forward, particularly by Edward Soja (1989, chapter 1), who traces the innate historicity of social theory to the Enlightenment discovery of progress and, specifically, to the nineteenth-century intellectual obsession with time. Hence social theory takes its place alongside biological evolution, science fiction novels, geological studies and Whig history as nineteenth-century 'time-centric' products bequeathed to the twentieth century. In the case of social theory, it is only since about 1985 that this legacy has been overcome and spatial concerns have moved to centre stage. The route taken is from space-as-platform, the stage upon which events take place (Foucault's 'dead space'), through space-as-context in which arrangement of things in space can have contingent influences, to space-as-structure or spatiality. The latter constitutes necessary socio-spatial relations, intrinsic to the institution or system under study. For instance, the inter-state system through its fragmentation of political power is deemed to be a necessary feature of the modern world-system, it is an element of its spatiality (Taylor, 1992). But there is much more to the 'geo' in a geohistorical perspective than identifying spatiality.

Where and what?

The English language is rich in words to answer where-and-what questions. In *Roget's Thesaurus* (Browning, 1986), for instance, 'Words relating to space' constitutes one of only six classes and is divided into 133 headings. This fecund lexicon has allowed the use of many terms to answer where-and-what questions in situations where space has entered social theory. Some terms are, however, more popular than others: the most common general term is 're-gion', which was once seen as the defining concept of geography but has been used widely throughout the social sciences. Other terms have become associated with particular studies; for reasons previously enunciated politics deals with territories, and, in addition, economics favours 'location' as in location theory, social studies have been concerned with 'areas' as in urban social areas, and in cultural studies 'landscapes' feature prominently. In recent years the concept of 'localities' has been developed, partly as a way of avoiding confusion consequent upon the above suite of where-and-what concepts. One term missing from the above list is 'place'. Probably as prevalent as space in common parlance, place is little used in social science but is to be found in humanities scholarship where, for instance, novels are often said to evoke particular places. I will suggest here that place and space are more primitive terms than the other concepts mentioned above. There is a sense in which the other terms can be reduced to either space or place: functional regions, economic locations and sovereign territories seem to qualify as spaces whereas homogeneous regions, urban social areas and cultural landscapes are more likely to be called places. But what is this 'sense'? Careful definition is in order.

The first point to make is that place and space are distinct and separate categories. This is necessary because several recent studies either ignore or blur the distinction. For instance, in his recent discussion of Henri Lefebvre's work on the production of space, Soja (1996, p. 40) explicitly eschews an interest in place as a concept on the grounds that any relevant aspects of the latter concept can be found within a sophisticated treatment of space as provided by Lefebvre. Similarly, two books with 'place' in their titles have not maintained a place–space distinction. John Urry's (1995, chapter 1) theoretical introduction to *Consuming Places* deals with only theoretical treatments of space. Presumably this implies that in dealing with space you are also considering place, that is to say, the terms are interchangeable. This is certainly the message of Rob Shields's (1991) *Places on the Margin*, whose key operating concept is 'social spatialization', despite a title emphasizing place, and who seems to use 'place-myth' and 'space-myth' as synonyms. I follow Yi-Fu Tuan (1977) in asserting that place and space are different.

But how do they differ? '"Space" is', according to Tuan (1977, p. 6), 'more abstract than "place".' This idea is basic to most understandings of the two terms, with space treated as general and place as particular: space is everywhere, place is somewhere. Moreover, place has content; the idea of an empty place is eerie, an empty space is merely geometrical. Tuan, however, is concerned for their relations: place as 'humanised space' (p. 54). This relates to Murray Bookchin's (1995) ideas on citizenship where, under the heading

'Urbanisation against cities', he contrasts the historical tradition of cities as places (political communities) with the contemporary spaces of bricks and mortar called urbanization. In this chapter I will focus upon this specific distinction between space and place, based upon abstraction.

The politics of this distinction are quite interesting. This can be appreciated by adding the adjective safe to each term: a safe place implies lots of people around, as famously described by Jane Jacobs (1961); a safe space is one monitored by cameras. In geopolitics there is spatial strategy which, at its crudest, in effect proclaims open season on places. Hence, general warfare is about one side attacking spaces while the other side defends places. Contrary to social theory, neither place nor space is 'dead'. The dynamism of place is in everyday behaviour, it is constituted by routinized movement; space is associated with the frontier and the movement of the explorer or pioneer who searches the spatial unknown. This is important because if time is added to the analysis the idea of transformation of space into place can be entertained. In the case of the frontier, as its location moves forward to the edge of new unknown spaces it leaves settled places behind. The best example of such a transformation occurs commonly in moving residence. The empty house or apartment which is inspected consists of spaces, functional rooms that have to be imagined as a potential home. It becomes the latter, a familiar place, when a new resident moves in and modifies the spaces to suit her or his needs in terms of content and decor. The idea of home is more than a familiar place, however. It can be much more intimate, even going as far as impinging directly on personal identity. This becomes clear in metaphoric uses of home at larger scales of activity: hometown and homeland are particularly special places because they encompass a politics of identity.

The last example highlights the fact that place can exist at different scales. This is not always the way place is interpreted. There is a widespread tendency to equate place with local. This leads to the idea of space as 'the stable framework that contains places' (Sack, 1992, p. 12). There is a good reason why places are often viewed as local: 'humanizing' space is most easily accomplished through micro face-to-face contacts. But there is no need to limit place creation to this one process, especially in political studies where the imagined community of the nation with its homeland place is central to so much research. Thus I follow Tuan's (1977, p. 149) contention that 'Place exists at different scales. At one extreme a favorite armchair is a place, at the other extreme the whole earth.' Of course, it is commonplace that space occurs at different scales, providing place with the same multiple-scale property means that relations between place and space can be explored beyond the local up to and including the geographical limit of the whole Earth as both place and space.

Place–space tensions

The above definitional exercise differs from much of the literature, especially in geography, which has often consisted of a place versus space debate; indeed the twentieth-century history of geography as a discipline can be viewed as the changing outcomes of such debate. I have chosen to study both together because I am interested in the relations between place and space rather than pitting the idea of one against the other. The key point is that the same location can be both place or space: everywhere, in fact, has the potential for being both place and space. This can be historical as when a space is transformed into a place or vice versa or it can be contemporaneous as when the same location is viewed from different perspectives. In practice these two processes merge in what I shall call *place–space tension* between the producers of space and the makers of place. I will interpret this as a particularly geographical expression of ambiguity within modernity. When place and space constitute a single entity they define a geographically focused, contested politics. The questions of who defines an institution in spatial terms and who sees it as a place create a modern politics of space and place.

I am going to use place–space tensions to add a critical edge to my previous discussion of home and state in chapters 3 and 4 respectively. Both chapters consisted largely of narratives tracing the changing nature of each institution without problematizing the outcomes in practice. As well as existing at different scales home and state represent a place and space respectively and both have 'modern partners' which complement them: household as space and nation as place. The two 'space' institutions, states and households, are particularly interesting geographically because their constitutive practices are embedded in bounded spaces of action, states defined by controlled-access territory and households defined by controlled-access residence respectively. These two institutions are as old as history itself but in the contemporary world they represent only half of a place–space tension.

Using modernist interpretations of nation and home, I argue that under conditions of modernity it has been found necessary to reinvent state as nation-state and household as home-household thus creating place–space tensions at the heart of the experience of being modern. Nation-state and home-household are modern humanized spaces. Building upon territorial behaviour focusing on defence, they have become geographical havens within modernity, intimate places which provide important elements of identity to modern human beings. This positive interpretation is complemented by negative uses of territoriality. The latter political strategy is never simply benign, the distribution of power within state and household ensures that the created nature of a given territory favours some at the expense of others. In fact, far from being a simple haven, both nation-state and home-household have been portrayed as a 'cage' for the mass of citizens and 'captive housewives' respectively. This is the tension which constitutes these very modern institutions.

One final point before I embark on drawing these place–space parallels – it is necessary to specify the position from which I will be assessing these two institutions. I consider whether each institution, first nation-state and then home-household, is enabling or dis-enabling from the general standpoint of progressive political movements such as those discussed in the previous chapter. The thesis I will be trying to illustrate is that, contrary to much radical thinking, places tend to be enabling and spaces to be dis-enabling. Put another way, this is Doreen Massey's (1993) idea of 'progressive places' writ large and accompanied by 'regressive spaces'.

Nation-state as enabling place and dis-enabling space

One of the obvious but little discussed features of the recent plethora of writings on geographical concepts and imaginations is a general tendency to focus more on space than place: a perusal of the indexes of 1990s general geography books (e.g. Livingstone, 1992;

Gregory, 1994; Johnston, 1997) will quickly confirm this. Being more abstract, space seems to be more amenable to discursive interrogation: from space we can derive spatial, spacious, spatialisation and spatiality but there are no placial, placious, placialization or placiality; these words are either deemed unnecessary, constitute immanent contradictions in terms, or have yet to be invented. There is also the suspicion implicit in much writing that the politics of place is inherently reactionary because of its association with localism. However, this has recently been given short shrift by Doreen Massey (1993; 1994) with her discussion of 'progressive places' as crossroads rather than bounded spaces. Whatever the reason for the spatial proclivity, political geography has been one exception to this rule. John Agnew (1987) and Ron Johnston (1991) have both focused explicitly on place as the central concept in their political studies. Johnston has been impressed by the continuity in the politics of places and provides a place-based cultural explanation for examples such as the Nottinghamshire coalfield's local resistance to national strike calls. The fact that a Marx versus Spencer political conflict was played out twice fifty-eight years apart (1926 and 1984) suggests to Johnston that there is something particular to this place and its coal community which is overriding both individual and national politics. Agnew's promotion of place is a direct assault on the embedded statism of social science which assumes homogeneous national cultures within which a national politics operates. Using Scottish and Italian examples, he shows that the implicit sovereign territorial spatiality of conventional political models completely fails to account for critical contemporary political changes which are inherently place-based. Hence, place is firmly on the agenda of current political geography research. But what of the relations between place and space? This is my concern here, giving precedence to neither place nor space.

I shall begin with the notion that space is more abstract than place, which immediately relates space to rationality, bureaucracy and the state. In this argument states are space-producers in their designation and recognition of boundaries. States impose spaces on places. The places being collected together or divided by the boundaries drawn by state elites are locations in which material life is reproduced in everyday routine behaviour. Interpreted as part of Fernand Braudel's (1980) *longue durée*, such places can be related to Johnston's concern for local culture but more generally they can become centres for resistance to state penetration. Spaces, therefore, are the outcome of top-down political processes; places can be the site for bottom-up opposition. But the world is not this simple; the political processes do not stop there. Although initially imposed, boundaries can themselves become familiar, become embedded in society and have their own effects on the reproduction of material life. In this way what were spaces are converted into places. A classic example would be the eighteenth-century English county as a place where 'polite' county society was reproduced within boundaries originally set out to demarcate a medieval sheriff's space of operation on behalf of the Crown.

The most important such space to place conversion, however, is the nation-state. As shown in chapter 4, in the modern world-system sovereign states existed long before the rise of nationalism. These states administered spaces – sovereign territories – created by a mixture of medieval legacy, dynastic alliances and military conquests. Although in early modern Europe small politico-military elites displayed some loyalty to these states, for the mass of those living in the state territory the state remained remote and, to the state, they were merely population to be counted and taxed within the territory. All this has changed in the last two hundred years. Nations have been constructed as imagined communities each with their own place in the world, their own homeland, some as 'fatherland', others as 'motherland'. By combining state and nation in nation-state, sovereign territory has been merged with sacred homeland to convert a space into the place. Notice that, given the scale, this is an 'imagined place' but is nevertheless reproduced in routine everyday behaviour which Michael Billig (1995) has famously called banal nationalism. Modern states are so powerful because they have become constructed as places out of spaces.

This conclusion provides a new perspective on the rise of the welfare state. Movements and parties which had had the overthrow of the state as their prime goal changed their direction as politics became nationalized. With the state becoming a place, it came to be seen as enabling, a powerful tool for carrying out a movement's political programme. Much radical debate in the late nineteenth century moved from how to overthrow the state to how to use it

(Taylor, 1991). This was the geographical basis of the first step towards the 'domestication of the left' described in the previous chapter. There was, however, one exception to this political transformation of the movements, the anarchists. They maintained that state politics was a political trap, that whatever the short-term attractions of an expanded franchise, in the long-term it would de-radicalize those who entered. This was a 'leopard does not change its spots' argument: becoming a national place made no difference to the fact that the state was fundamentally dis-enabling, a de-humanizer of places as a producer of spaces.

In the twentieth century states have tried hard to prove the anarchists were right. Legitimated as places, states have continued as producers of spaces. This can be traced to the very origins of the nation-state. France after the Revolution was the first modern state to designate its territory as sacred but this creation of France as a place was at the expense of existing sub-national places. The administrative reorganization of France was accomplished by eliminating all existing sub-units and replacing them by arbitrary equal-area hexagons as *départements* of the state. To consolidate the elimination of places by these new spaces no traditional names were given to departments, indeed labelling the *départements* was avowedly anti-social: they were named after local physical features, notably rivers and hills. Of course, states, even revolutionary ones, are not powerful enough to convert everyday reproduction in manifold places into a single place; multiple 'local Frances' continued under the national umbrella. Nevertheless, states dividing up their territory into arbitrary political units named after physical features to eliminate places as potential sites of political resistance has continued into the twentieth century – inter-war Romania and Yugoslavia have been documented in some detail by political geographers (Helin, 1967; Poulsen, 1971).

States have been more successful in eliminating places in their imperial and frontier expansions. Worlds of non-European places were converted into new worlds of European spaces. As well as being 'peoples without history' (Wolf, 1982), the occupants of these areas into which Europeans moved were also converted into peoples without geography. They and their places were invisible to the state surveyors and cartographers carving up the 'empty space'. The resulting geometrical divisions of other worlds have been termed

'antecedent boundaries' by Richard Hartshorne (1936). Antecedent to whom? Us, of course: Hartshorne's terminology neatly con-
firms the removal of geography from non-European peoples. The
evidence for this spatial elimination of places stares out at us every
time we look at the extra-Europeans portions of the world political
map where Europeans have held or do hold power. The straight
lines that carve up the maps of Australia, Africa, Canada and the
USA all bear witness to the space creation of states. And, of course,
with 'empty spaces', there is no choice but to find new names for
these newly bounded spaces, often in non-social terms: physical
features – compass points, rivers and hills – abound as the first
stage in imprinting the new on the old.

Although never implemented, there is a famous proposal for
Europe to receive some of its own medicine. The incident I am
thinking about is the 'great map scandal' of 1942 when the American geographer George Renner advocated a top-down carve up of
Europe with little or no regard for the wishes of the inhabitants
(DeBres, 1986). From his privileged outsider location in New York,
Renner viewed the non-American world as a space ripe for reorganization for its own good as defined by him. In the case of
Europe, Renner employs a crude balance of power argument to
advocate a peace based upon large states with the consequent
elimination of all small states. Lines are drawn across the map of
Europe in a manner not dissimilar to what Europeans did to other
continents. Protesters did not seem to appreciate the irony of their
defence of places for Europeans, the great imperial destroyers of
places elsewhere.

This state predilection to convert places into spaces is not just
a historical phenomenon, as I suggested at the beginning of this section, it is inherent in the bureaucratic nature of state practices. Efficiency in administrative theory can only be achieved by converting
messy places into rational spaces. Whereas the former vary in size
and in spacing, the latter demand approximately equal-size zones in
both area and population. Hence spaces continue to be imposed on
places. Local government reform in England has been a typical example. It is necessary to have a geographical imagination by-pass
operation in order to create the space called Sefton as a combination
of the places Bootle and Southport. The reformers' problem was
that in 1974 Liverpool was already oversize by the given criterion

and with Southport undersize there was only one way for Bootle to go. The give-away for examples of this disrespect for the nature of place can be found in the need to invent new names to cover the deficiency in geographical imagination. How many people in England outside its surrounding area know where Halton (a space with a population of more than 100,000) is? It is in new Cheshire, created by combining old Lancashire's Widnes with Cheshire's Runcorn. Examples such as this could be multiplied many times over but there is another indication of disrespect for place I wish to note: the proliferation of designated 'boroughs' covering large swathes of rural land. For instance, on travelling north on the Great North Road you enter the 'Borough of Berwick-upon-Tweed' just north of the town of Alnwick, some twenty miles from the town of Berwick itself. Similarly the 'Borough of Macclesfield' is entered just off the M6 with some twenty miles of Cheshire countryside to go through before you reach the place most people would identify as Macclesfield. Where I work, the administrative space is called the 'Borough of Charnwood', which presumably shows somebody had difficulty distinguishing old forests from modern towns such as Loughborough. These spaces remain from the 1970s 'modernization' of the British state, but the administrative counties named after rivers have been sunk: Avon, Humberside, Teesside, Tyne and Wear, spaces given and then taken away and hardly noticed.

I think this inherent bureaucratic nature of the state has been the main reason that it has proved impossible to reform English local government to reflect the day-to-day lives of the people. This point was made most explicitly in Derek Senior's 'Memorandum of Dissent' to the Redcliffe-Maud Report on local government reform in the late 1960s (Honey, 1981, pp. 253–5). He disagreed with his colleagues on the Royal Commission and was unable to persuade them that 'to define the functional requirements and then find interaction areas consistent with functional needs' (p. 254) was to approach the problem fundamentally the wrong way round. From Derek Senior to the current city region campaign (City Region Campaign, 1996), trying to get the British state to respect places and eschew spaces has proved to be impossible. In this respect it is a dis-enabling state. More generally, whether revolutionary, authoritarian, imperial or liberal-democratic, creating spaces is what states do, home and away.

Home-household as enabling place and dis-enabling space

As I described in chapter 3, the bourgeoisies of the hegemons have been at the forefront of creating the modern home. That argument intersects here with Yi-Fu Tuan's (1977) description of the home as the intimate place. I return to Witold Rybczynski's (1986) short history of the home from which I drew the notion of the home as an enabling institution, a haven from modernity's turmoils. Now I can add a further dimension to the argument: I search out the other side of the home-household, its propensity to be dis-enabling for women.

In defining a boundary between public and private worlds the Dutch invented domesticity (Rybczynski, 1986, p. 75). Of course this was not the first gender division of labour but the 'feminization of the home' (p. 72) did create a new isolation of women's work (p. 71). Rybczynski (pp. 74–5) interprets this as enabling for women as the house changed to become 'a feminine place, or at least under feminine control' (see also Hufton, 1995, pp. 47–8). This 'central position of the woman in the Dutch household' (Rybczynski, 1986 p. 74) was accompanied by married women of all social positions carrying out their own day-to-day household chores in a manner which can be interpreted as liberating (p. 72). And all this can be viewed in the domestic genre of seventeenth-century Dutch painting:

> During the Renaissance, when women had been solitary figures in a painting, it was as Madonnas, saints or biblical personages, the Dutch painters were the first to choose ordinary women as their subjects. It was natural for women to be the focus of de Witte's paintings, because the domestic world that he was depicting had become *their* realm. The world of male work, and male social life, had moved elsewhere. The house had become the place for another kind of work – specialized domestic work – women's work. . . . When a male is included in a Vermeer, one has the sense that he is a visitor – an intruder – for these women do not simply inhabit these rooms, they occupy them completely. Whether they are sewing, playing the spinet or reading a letter, the Dutch women are solidly, emphatically, contentedly at home. (Rybczynski, 1986, pp. 70–1)

But perhaps it was not quite as simple as this. The last line of the quotation brings to mind Gillian Rose's (1993, p. 56) criticism of humanistic geographers' cosy interpretation of the home: 'only masculinist work could use the image of place as home so unproblematically'. And, of course, the image of the Dutch home bequeathed to us by Dutch genre painting is a male one: painters were organized into city guilds with apprenticeships restricted to boys (Kahr, 1993, p. 11). Hence the women's contentedness in the pictures is a male creation, women's images of the home are simply not available. As well as enabling as a woman's place, the home has been interpreted as a specific constraint on women achieving their individual potential which is not faced by men. In this way the new spatial gender division of labour may have produced home as a refuge for men but, equally, it may have constituted a new prison for women: as 'the space of the home' it becomes dis-enabling (Oakley, 1974, p. 32). I would argue that, like the state, the household is a politically ambiguous institution, both enabling and dis-enabling. Home was created as both place and space.

The construction of 'English comfort' included the creation of the 'drawing room' – to which women 'withdrew' after dinner – the first place where 'comfortable chairs' could be drawn up to the fire (Rybczynski, 1986, pp. 117–18). But the critical effect of British industrial-ization was to remove large numbers of households away from rural means of daily reproduction. This process culminated in the separation of work and home penetrating through into the working classes as men struggled for a 'family wage' so that women were released from the labour market, their free domestic labour being used to create a comfortable home life (Mackenzie and Rose, 1983, pp. 161–7). By the end of the nineteenth century this separation was consolidated through the twin ideological concepts of thrift and respectability as lower middle- and working-class women created the classic Victorian home. But, as Suzanne Mackenzie and Damaris Rose (1983, p. 164) have pointed out, this female achievement was an ambiguous one: 'For working-class men, the home had become a necessary haven. For their wives, however, no such separation (between work and home) existed. The home was primarily their workplace, and in some ways it had become a more oppressive one.' Again the home-household tension defined both an enabling place and a dis-enabling space.

Consumer modernity has had a profound, but changing, effect on the home-household as both enabling and dis-enabling. Rybczynski (1986, p. 161) reminds us that 'when electricity entered the home, it was by the kitchen door'. The new consumption was based initially upon the growth of consumer durables which every modern home had to have. With these new appliances, domestic work became legitimated as home *economics* or domestic *science*, and women experienced a degree of power and control reminiscent of their Dutch sisters three centuries earlier. Rybczynski (1986, pp. 160–1) argues that the 'masculine idea' of the home as a sedentary haven was replaced by a more dynamic feminine idea of the home in the new American-style suburbs. But, again, there was another side to this enabling place. Now more than ever, many women were condemned to an inherently lonely existence, doubly separated – first in the home and second in the suburb. Instead of concentrated comfort, the suburb was seen as a space isolated from the rest of the world. Like the state, the household could become a 'cage', in this case occupied by the 'captive wife' (Gavron, 1966). The spatial isolation of the newly constructed 'housewife' became a major source of 'job dissatisfaction' (Oakley, 1974, pp. 100–1). This mid-twentieth-century phenomenon has been partly alleviated by the increasing level of consumption having to be paid for through two wages, giving women a dual role as 'part breadwinners' but often still full-time domestic workers: women no longer so lonely but very tired in the late twentieth century (Mackenzie and Rose, 1983, pp. 175–6).

In conclusion I wish to make one important point: the two place–space tensions are not independent processes. My separate treatments of nation-states and home-households have been for pedagogic reasons only since their recent histories are intimately intertwined. They come together most explicitly in the USA with the Hoover Report of 1931 where government, bankers, manufacturers and builders agreed that new urbanization through single-family dwelling units (home-households) would be a long-term solution to the Depression (of the nation-state) because it maximized consumption (Hayden, 1981, p. 23). The great irony is that this national economic growth imperative through home consumption practices leads ultimately to a new, much larger, place–space tension between the Earth as an ecological place and the world as an economic space. I will return to this in the Epilogue.

7

Americanization

The idea of the twentieth century as America's century is as old as the century itself. As early as 1899 the Pope was explicitly condemning 'Americanism' and two years later a book appeared with the title *The Americanization of the World* (Vann Woodward, 1991, p. 81). But the concept of the 'American Century' is indelibly linked to Henry Luce, the editor of *Life* magazine, writing to support the USA's entry into World War II in 1941. Later turned into a book with commentaries (Luce, 1941), his statement laying out America's relationship with the rest of the world is a truly remarkable historical document. It marks a gestalt switch from America the pure and isolated to America the active proselytizer.

Reading Luce's words more than half a century on, one is struck by the immense confidence he displays in America's ability to determine the rest of the world's future. This is not typical nationalist war-time bravado; it is as if Luce had had access to Gramsci's Prison Notebooks and was projecting his ideas on hegemony to the world stage. Luce displays a hegemonic temper in the sense that he is concerned with so much more than winning the immediate war. In Gramscian terms, Luce's article is an international case being made for 'moral and intellectual leadership'. For instance, Luce claims that 'we can make a truly *American* internationalism something as natural to us in our time as the airplane or the radio' (1941, p. 26, emphasis in original). I agree completely with one of the commentators in *The American Century* who draws a direct parallel between Luce's arguments and earlier pronouncements of British statesmen in the way in which 'he has achieved . . . complete identification of his own nation's interests with the interests of humanity and of moral law' (p. 56). In almost a parody of his own American nationalism, he calls for 'an internationalism of the people, by the people and for the people' (p. 33). In this way he expressly rejects the role of world policeman for America and opts instead to influence the 'world environment . . . for the growth of American life' (pp. 23–4). Since winning World War II did lead directly into a period commonly recognized as American hegemony, Luce's article can be viewed as truly portentous.

Using a mixture of historical narrative and political analysis, in this chapter I consider both the changing nature of Americanization and the conditions for its success as a new pervasive modernity. This is, therefore, a case study of one of the prime modernities, putting some flesh on the skeletal descriptions presented previously. Obviously I have chosen to focus on processes behind consumer modernity because it is the experience of all my readers. Of course, Americanization is not as straightforward as the popular terms Cocacolarization, McWorld and Disnification suggest. As well as emulation there is envy, but also where there is coercion there is admiration. My favourite slogan remains that recorded on a central American wall where under the familiar 'Yankee Go Home' somebody had added 'And Take Me with You'.

Incipient, capacious and resonant Americanizations

After World War II Germany was subjected to a propaganda onslaught by the four occupying powers as they sought 'denazification' in their quite distinctive and separate ways (FitzGibbon, 1969). In his account of the US occupation, Ralph Willett (1989, 27) makes a curious observation: 'the Occupation (and its Americanization potential) succeeded best when it stopped trying.' It seems that 'Americanization of young Germans was much more successful outside the schools' (p. 17). This was because it was not teachers or administrators or soldiers or any other public servants who promoted America best; rather, 'It was American goods which were to be the revolutionary missionaries for the American Way of Life' (p. 27). What is happening here is the projection of a civil society rather than the state itself. Even in the strict political conditions of a military occupation and state reconstruction, the dominating force is the 'non-political' appeal of America.

This unusual circumstance is quintessentially hegemonic. There were particular processes unfolding in the American zone of defeated Germany which actualized a much deeper effect than the political domination, however complete the latter. American influence in Germany was beginning to transform the cultural matrix of society by penetrating the everyday lives of the German people. This had nothing to do with the occupation *per se*, but was a much wider process which could be found equally in victor states such as Britain and France. I will define Americanization as this projection of American civil society to create a new general form of modernity. As integral to world hegemony, Americanization should develop in line with the phases of the American hegemonic cycle. I identify, therefore, three manifestations of Americanization: incipient Americanization is part of the rise phase; capacious Americanization is the process at high hegemony; and during the demise phase there is a resonant Americanization. These three Americanizations are described chronologically.

There is a discrepancy between the rise of American political power and the influence of its civil society in the first half of the twentieth century. The USA began the century as recent victors in the American-Spanish war and their growing political influence culminated in entry into World War I, victory and the creation of the League of Nations as a US project. Defeat for President Wilson in 1920, however, marked the onset of a political isolationism by which the USA forsook world leadership. In contrast, it was in the 1920s that American cultural influence came to the fore. This was the period when American film stars like Charlie Chaplin, Mary Pickford and Douglas Fairbanks became household names across the world. Alongside this 'invasion of Hollywood', America was to make its first major foray into dominating popular music through the international spread of jazz. Important as these cultural products were, there was something even more basic to this incipient Americanization.

It seemed as if, in the 1920s, the USA was creating a new type of society. Lukacs (1993, p. 145) characterizes the changes in terms of the 'shape' of society from pyramid (i.e. with a base consisting of many poor people) to onion-shaped, implying a majority of middle-income people. Inevitably this was associated with fundamental changes in the everyday lives of Americans. Higher wages were reflected in more consumption especially in the home. This was the time when Americans consumed over half the world's electricity, much of it through new 'gadgets' in the home. Hence the birth of the new suburban lifestyle centred on the home as the locus of consumer durables. As well as indirectly through film, these domestic developments came to the notice of the outside world in two main ways. While other countries were developing their propaganda arm of the state with 'official' cultural institutions, Americanization proceeded through essentially private means: the production and marketing of American corporations, and visitors' reports and letters home from immigrants (Duignan and Gann, 1992, pp. 420–1). (The State Department only set up a cultural relations division in 1938 and Voice of America only began broadcasting in 1942 as part of the war effort.) Incipient Americanization was clearly not a public project, which was unthinkable in a period of US political isolationism. But the American message got through nevertheless via the two 'unofficial' media.

First, with increased economic protectionism, the fast-growing American corporations were forced to set up production behind the tariff barriers. In Europe, Germany became the main US economic base with ITT, General Motors and IG Chemicals leading the way. Coca-Cola opened its factory in Essen in 1929. In Britain, this is the period when a host of companies which were to become famous household brand names built factories: for example, Hoover, Gillette, McLeans, Remington, Firestone and Ford (Marling, 1993, p. 106). The market for consumer goods still lagged far behind America but the beginnings of the new modernity were being put into place. Second, as letters from immigrants and reports from visitors began to filter through to other civil societies, leading intellectuals came to suspect that they were being provided with a glimpse of a new world. While Antonio Gramsci, writing in 1929 and intrigued by the high wage regime of the USA, was wondering whether the 'new culture' and 'way of life' represented 'a new beacon of civilization' or merely 'a new coating' on European civilization (Hoare and Smith, 1971, pp. 317–18), Jean-Paul Sartre had no such doubts: 'Skyscrapers were the architecture of the future, just as the cinema was the art and jazz the music of the future' (Duignan and Gann, 1992, p. 410).

Duignan and Gann (1992, p. 409) identify the 1940s as a 'sea change' in American society, with confidence in the 'American Way' replacing an earlier 'mood of cultural deference' when educated Americans automatically looked to Europe for their cultural lead. This confidence was quite pervasive. At the end of World War II only the USA assumed the good times were coming; Ellwood (1992, p. 21) reports Keynes's surprise on encountering American optimism at Bretton Woods. As the arsenal and financier of war victory, America was now in a special position to project itself across the spectrum of social relations – political, cultural and economic. This is high hegemony, the period when the rest of the world is offered a comprehensive societal package. It is capacious Americanization.

Today, when Americanization is often viewed in narrow cultural terms, it is important to emphasize that the projection of the American Way of Life at mid-century was based upon production processes more than anything else. The technology leadership of US industry – 'American know-how' – meant that American workers were producing two to five times as much per day as European workers (Price, 1955, p. 328). It is not surprising, therefore, that although the Marshall Plan began by emphasizing the need to raise gross production, it soon changed to focus upon raising productivity. In this way reconstruction came to be viewed as the 'modernization of European industry' which in turn brought the 'growth idea' to the centre of decision-making. Institutions were set up to take managers and workers on visits to the USA so that they could learn the new and better ways of production at first hand. It was at this time (1950–2) that France sent forty such missions to the USA and, according to Kuisel (1993, p. 84), discovered 'management' as opposed to traditional French 'direction'. All this created a new politics based upon economic growth leading to higher levels of consumption and thus voter contentment (Ellwood, 1992, p. 94). This Americanization was to privilege class compromise over class conflict in new political reconstructions in all Western European states, as I described in chapter 5.

In many ways the real test case for the power of capacious Americanization was France under President de Gaulle. As an arch opponent of American hegemony, he promoted security and economic policies to lessen US influence in Europe. But the paradox was that it was the decade of the 1960s, at the very height of de Gaulle's power, that coincided with rampant Americanization within France itself (Kuisel, 1993, chapter 6). This is best represented by Jean-Jacques Servan-Schreiber's best-selling book of 1967 which advocated the opposite of de Gaulle: accommodation to American power rather than insulation from it. After extolling the prowess of US multinational corporations, he proposes, in Arthur Schlesinger's (1968, p. x) term, a 'discriminating Americanization' focusing on organization as an alternative to an 'easy temptation to Americanization' by simple employment of Americans to manage French industry (Servan-Schreiber, 1968, p. 27). The high point of this type of thinking came with John Ney's (1970) appropriately entitled book *The European Surrender,* where he argues that 'Americans are on top because they are intrinsically different' (p. 10), they are 'the only people who can *cope* with technological living at the American level' (p. 6). Nevertheless, Europeans will try their best to emulate their superiors (p. 12) because 'the European present can only duplicate the American past' (p. 4). This Americanization argument for 'a predetermined future' (p. 5) represents an ideological zenith of this particular hegemonic cultural domination.

Ironically, Ney's book appeared just as the material conditions that gave it its credibility were disappearing. After 1970 other countries' corporations began seriously to rival the original US multinationals and the idea of a 'productivity gap' became as likely to refer to American inferiority as superiority. This coincided with a change in the way people began to interpret the new modernity. Kuisel (1993, p. 6) identifies 1970 as the watershed with, as he sees it, new social change becoming 'increasingly disconnected from America . . . it would be better described as the coming of consumer society' (p. 4). For instance, in terms of the radical ideas associated with the 1968 revolution in France, 'America became less the perpetrator of some universal crime and more a fellow victim of a global dynamic' (Kuisel, 1993, p. 186). But Americanization was too embedded in the everyday lives of Europeans simply to disappear with American high hegemony.

The oddity of Americanization is that it is more visible today than during its high point. Whereas a previous generation experienced Americanization at the cinema or on TV, now it can be encountered directly in any high street as numerous burger, chicken or pizza fast food joints. It is sometimes forgotten how recent this development is: the first McDonald's did not open in Britain until 1974. Marling (1993, p. 15) interprets this contemporary Americanization as 'set firmly in a timewarp': 'it's about nostalgia because it is not America *now* that we're in love with, but America as it was when it first swept us off our feet in the 1950s.' Cowboy films may no longer be popular but things American remain fascinating to new generations of Europeans (Marling, 1993, p. 7). This is a resonant Americanization reverberating into our present.

Inside America: conditions for constructing a modernity

A problem with structurally ordered narratives such as that above is that they tend to suggest an inevitable continuity in the sequence of events covered. This is a general implication I do not want to be assumed here. World hegemony is a contested project and not just in terms of world war. Hegemony requires a relatively high level of domestic consensus as a stable home base from which to project power and this has to be constructed. And, of course, there has to be a positive will to promote such projection; a hegemonic internationalism has to be constructed as a bipartisan foreign policy. There is nothing inevitable about either of these preconditions for a successful hegemonic project. In addition, they have to operate together as a domestic–international nexus in order to generate the immense momentum required for constructing a new modernity. Obviously, the key period for these constructions is either side of the turnover from the hegemonic rise phase to high hegemony. Hence, here I focus upon the two decades from 1933 to 1952, from the start of the New Deal to the end of the Marshall Plan.

The consensus politics that laid the stable foundations for the great economic boom of the early post-war decades has the generic title of corporatism. As an alternative to the designation 'American', the twentieth century has been called 'the century of corporatism' (O'Sullivan, 1988). In the 1920s Republican Herbert Hoover's concept of the 'associative state' to stimulate economic growth by co-operation between government and business was the first major step towards an American corporatism but was lost to the Great Depression (Hogan, 1987, pp. 23–9). With Roosevelt's New Deal a more interventionist corporatism was envisaged initially but Supreme Court defeats led to a regulatory corporatism that was to serve the USA well when the depression was over. In this the USA differed from its Western allies, where corporatism was constructed as various types of social and christian democracy. These more interventionist state corporatisms had the potential for autarchic foreign policies, anathema to hegemony, but this did not materialize. How did the weak corporatism of the USA accommodate these stronger versions into its hegemonic project?

The US corporatism that had emerged by the 1920s was built upon ideas of scientific management whereby increased productivity was supposed to boost both profit and wages. The latter was expected to create the demand for the increased production in a virtuous circle of economic growth. But as well as creating consumers, mass production eliminated craftsmen and so critically reduced the power of the leading unions (Rupert, 1995, p. 60). Hence, although the virtuous circle seemed to be working for a short period, the enhanced power inequalities at the workplace soon had deleterious effects. Wages did not keep pace with inflation in the 1920s and therefore the necessary mass consumption to complement the mass production did not materialize (p. 79). The political balance of power changed after 1932 with the unions as part of Roosevelt's victorious coalition. New industrial unions emerged to challenge the corporations in a series of great recognition conflicts which enabled labour to emerge as important, albeit junior, partners in the post-war corporatism. In a series of key strikes and negotiations, high wages ushered in the mass consumption whose absence had brought down 1920s corporatism (p. 97). No longer opposing enhanced productivity, the role of American unions came to be to ensure their members got a fair share of the subsequent spoils so that they could become middle-class consumers. These were the basic social relations that provided the domestic consensus upon which American hegemony could be projected to the rest of the world.

American unions were directly instrumental in this projection. As integral to the new 'hegemonic bloc', they operated in Western Europe to promote US-style social relations through supporting 'non-political' unionism. For instance, American union leaders contributed to the Marshall Plan as labour advisers and were particularly involved in the new productivity initiatives (Rupert, 1995, p. 51). But these 'non-political' union bosses were also highly political in their anti-communism. They worked with US Intelligence to split French and Italian national trade union organizations in order to isolate the communists (p. 48). Their greatest success came in 1949 with the splitting of the World Federation of Trade Unions and the setting up of the International Confederation of Free Trade Unions. This brought non-communist unions in Western Europe into the US hegemonic bloc committed to productivity and trade to furnish high wages.

The rise of American corporatism was complemented by the development of a bilateral internationalism of the main political parties. For each hegemon, there has been one particular political grouping that have been the main supporters of the internationalism necessary to promote hegemonic power (Taylor, 1996a, p. 117). The classic 'hegemonic party' was the British Liberal Party but the Dutch 'States Party' with its peace policy played a similar, earlier internationalist role. For the USA, the Democratic Party were the liberal internationalists. However, world hegemony cannot proceed with its premises contested within the domestic politics. Hegemony is established only when the 'opposition party' falls into line and accepts the hegemonic agenda. This conversion can be traced in the Dutch 'Orangeist Party' and the British Conservatives; for America it is represented by the movement of the Republicans in the 1940s from isolationism to full support of the Cold War with its worldwide interventionist implications.

In 1940 the Republican Party was split with the Presidential nomination going to Wendell Willkie, an internationalist who had written a popular book, *One World*, which presaged much of what was to become American hegemonic policy. Other leading Republicans such as Henry Luce, Paul Hoffman and Averill Harriman were being drawn into public international positions – the latter two along with Mrs Wendell Willkie were to hold important positions in the administration of the Marshall Plan. But in Congress many Republicans remained staunchly isolationist behind their leader Senator Arthur Vandenburg. Later he was to say that isolationism ended with Pearl Harbor but the latter event was not necessarily a good reason to support a post-war internationalist policy. In fact the end of the war was quickly followed by a demobilization which implied global disengagement. Furthermore, Truman's policy of opening up the markets of the British Empire through its loan conditions was soon in difficulties in Congress. The Democrat administration might be pursuing a 'one world' policy for the benefit of American business in search of markets but this was threatened by a revival of American suspicion of internationalist policy (Taylor, 1990). Anti-communism came to the rescue. With the promotion of the Truman Doctrine, Vandenburg was carefully cultivated by the State Department and his support was crucial. A similar process operated with respect to the Marshall Plan. Remobilization for the Korean War consolidated the anti-communism and the Cold War meant that American business had finally about two-thirds of the world open to it. By the time the Republicans returned to the White House after a twenty-year gap, in 1953, there was no possibility that the USA would not have an international interventionist policy. The emphases in foreign policy would differ but the hegemonic party policy agenda would stay on course: hegemonic bipartisan internationalism was in place.

Quite clearly, the common thread in these two constructions which finally incorporated both unions and isolationists firmly in the hegemonic camp was anti-communism. This is a particular expression of a general hegemonic practice. All three hegemons have ideologically built their self-identity as champions of 'freedom' against an unfree Other: Dutch republicanism against royal tyrants (absolutism), British liberal constitutionalism against eastern despots (orientalism), and now American democracy against communist dictators (totalitarianism) (Taylor, 1996a, chapter 2). It is in this way that the political link is made between the distinctive nature of a hegemonic domestic politics and its given international context. Thus there is a continuing ideological concern for 'freedom' at the heart of the nexuses that link the domestic to the international in hegemonic projects, and the USA has been no exception.

Outside America: seeing the most modern of the modern

The Marshall Plan, in Imanuel Wexler's (1983, p. 254) opinion, when tested against the economic realities of 1952 could be considered 'only a qualified success'. But as the 1950s progressed and the post-war boom spread across the Atlantic, the Plan came to be hailed 'as one of the great economic success stories of modern time' (p. 255). As parts of the world began to Americanize, Americans became concerned to trace how their domination of the 'free world' was being received among the general populations of other countries. As a sign of the times, this was the first hegemon to be concerned for its image! One consequence was the setting up of a project by the American European Foundation of New York to elicit opinions on the USA by selected essayists from twenty countries covering all five continents. It is not clear what the basis of selection was except for geographical spread within the 'free world' and first-hand experience of being in America. All essayists were given the same letter of invitation in which they were asked both to provide their view and to assess the views of their country's people towards the USA. The essays were completed in late 1957 and early 1958 and were published a year later under the title *As Others See Us: The United States through Foreign Eyes* (Joseph, 1959). Albeit unrepresentative elite views and assessments, nonetheless this publication gives a unique insight into foreign reactions to American hegemony at its height. *As Others See Us* is an extremely useful source on the nature of the receptive audience for Americanization outside the USA and the following discussion is based solely on this unusual collection of essays.

Although the contributors to *As Others See Us* are quite diverse in their backgrounds and experiences, the editor considers it to be 'striking' that 'they show a large measure of agreement with one another in what they say about the United States' (Joseph, 1959, p. vi). I agree very much with this interpretation and consider the communality of opinion to be direct evidence of the success of the hegemonic project. In what follows I begin by showing how the image of America as a new modern world is expressed before looking at the evidence of how this image was contested.

I consider the following observation to be the quintessence of what it means to experience the modern.

> What interested me in the United States . . . was the 'modern' concept, in which all things seemed to be done in a revolutionary 'modern' way. Everything was the product of fresh thinking, from the foundations up. Everything had been 'improved', and was continually being 'improved' from day to day, almost from hour to hour. The restlessness, mobility, the increasing quest for something better impressed me. (Barzini, 1959, p. 73)

This was the impression of an Italian immigrant who landed in the USA in 1925. But such ideas are by no means limited to the optimistic image of an immigrant; ideas of a new modern world permeate the whole volume of essays. For instance, from England we are told that the USA is 'the model progressive society' (Brogan, 1959, p. 24); the French essayist is struck 'above all' 'by the originality of American society' (Aron, 1959, p. 58); from Switzerland we are presented with 'America the symbol of the up-to-date twentieth century, of the brave new world' (Freymond, 1959, p. 83); and finally, the German essayist holds 'an image of the American as being from another world' (Zahn, 1959, p. 97). These ideas are complemented by many references to America as the future: according to the essayist from Indonesia 'you have the feeling that in the United States you are on the threshold of the future' (Lubis, 1959, p. 204) and the South African writer thinks that the USA represents 'the seed and kernel of the future' (Broughton, 1959, p. 263). All these ideas are brought together by the essayist from pre-communist Cuba in another quintessential image of what it is to be modern: 'America signifies above all else a *new* world . . . in being a world *for the new* . . . not merely the land of the future . . . It means a *vocation for newness*, an openness for rectification and creation' (Manach, 1959, p. 340, emphasis in the original).

This is all a very impressive testament to the modernity of America but two essayists from outside Western Europe actually go further, to distinguish the USA from a past European modernity. The writer from Yugoslavia refers to 'how vastly the US differs from the industrialized countries of Western Europe' (Yilfan, 1959, p. 119), and from Indonesia the idea that 'American capitalism is no longer recognizable as the capitalist monster of the nineteenth century' (Lubis, 1959, p. 200) is presented. Later this author compares America directly with Europe and considers the world centre of culture to have been transferred to the former (p. 204).

And yet with all this upheaval and change, America offers a programme for taming the very dynamism it is unleashing on the world. This is very neatly picked up by the Swiss essayist, who identifies the ordinary stability to be found in the American home:

> This America of everyday life is simple and accessible ... It is a modern land where technical ingenuity is apparent at every point, in the equipment of the kitchen as well as of the car, but at the same time a land of gardens, of flowers, of home activities, where a man, away from his office or his work-place, enjoys tinkering at his bench, making a piece of furniture, repainting his house, repairing a fence, or mowing his lawn. A land of luxury but also of simple pleasures. (Freymond, 1959, p. 84)

This remarkable homage to American suburbia as modernity for ordinary people illustrates the popular basis for the success of Americanization.

There are plenty of references to copying the USA in *As Others See Us*, with the Latin American commentators perhaps least critical. According to the Cuban essayist 'one must recognize that today it is one of the most noble and attractive abiding places that man has yet been able to build for himself' so that 'There is much in it that other nations can take as an example' (Manach, 1959, p. 339). According to the Mexican essayist 'there is not a single country that does not aspire to be like the United States' (Villegas, 1959, p. 292). This can be contrasted with essays that are anti-Americanization. In contradiction to all other commentators, the writer from Fascist Spain sees Americans as merely modified Europeans with 'a lack of originality', 'an incapacity for creation' and an 'intellectual inferiority' so that America offers 'nothing new or compelling' (Marias, 1959, p. 26). And from the Philippines, an American colony little more than a decade earlier, the essay refers to those embracing America as 'cultural renegades' (Castrence, 1959, p. 235). But most commentators stand between these opposite positions of love and hatred, or at least mix them up, epitomized by the English statement that 'all the free world envies, copies, admires and fears' America (Brogan, 1959, p. 24).

The question is, who is doing the admiring and who is doing the fearing? In fact the essays in *As Others See Us* are generally very good at showing the contested nature of Americanization. There are clear class and generational differences in reactions to American hegemony. The former is particularly well expressed in the English essay as we might expect. While the 'British working classes proved scandalously avid for the material gains of the American way of life', for the elite 'it was smart to ignore America' (Brogan, 1959, pp. 16–17). Hence here emulation is given a very ungracious twist: 'Outwardly despised, America was, in England as in the rest of the world, from China to Peru, the successful material society to be imitated, with whatever gestures of moral repulsion' (p. 19). But the popular will of the mass of the English has triumphed and the anti-Americans 'have been reluctantly forced to notice that the very aspects of the American way of life that they despise are those most treasured, envied, and emulated by the mass of the British people' (p. 24). The essay from France makes very much the same point (Aron, 1959, p. 66). This can be interpreted as the classes who did well out of the old modernity despising the success of the new because it is turning their world upside down. And it is the new modernity which is particularly attractive to the new generation – for instance according to the essayist from Turkey 'the appeal of the American way of life seems strongest among the young generation in cities' (Sarc, 1959, p. 146).

But the key point is the mass appeal of Americanization. The Spanish essayist is particularly insightful on this. He identifies the paradox that US workers are the most affluent in the world and yet the USA is anathema to the political left. It is, he says, 'as if the American workers were not actually workers' (Marias, 1959, p. 34). Precisely: the American way of life resulted from converting workers into middle-class consumers, that is, the essence of the new consumer modernity. But the most prescient contribution is that of Raymond Aron. Although Americanization in France is looked upon by some 'with horror', he queries whether it is rather more universal than a 'battle . . . against Americanism'. He asks whether French experience in the 1950s is 'the universalizing of phenomena linked to the development of material civilization' in general (Aron, 1959, p. 60). Aron is ambiguous in his answer. He wonders whether France will 'become a mediocre replica of the United States?' (p. 70) but he also broaches the idea that France is becoming a new France for a new modernity while remaining as French as ever, as a later commentator was to put it (Kuisel, 1993, p. 237). This conclusion can be generalized beyond France to how American hegemony transformed the world-system: each country 'negotiated' its own Americanization within the new consumer modernity.

Americanization and globalization

The attraction of things American has not necessarily diminished with the onset of the demise phase of the American hegemonic cycle. As noted in the discussion of resonant Americanization, the impact of the USA on other societies is visually more apparent today. However, McDonaldization, Disnification, Cocacolarization, the Levi generation and so on have come to be interpreted as much as symptoms of globalization as Americanization *per se*. The obvious explanation for this is that a transformation of Americanization into globalization has occurred, signifying the ultimate success of the former. Certainly specific Americanization has become a more general consumerism – that is the way in constructing a prime modernity. But it would be misleading to suggest globalization is a simple extension of Americanization and not just because globalization is promoted by non-American as much as by American corporations.

Globalization is different in kind from Americanization. Despite the obvious corporate continuities in the examples given above, globalization belongs to a different time. The key point is that during high hegemony the USA spread an air of social optimism in keeping with the mammoth self-confidence, some would say arrogance, of a hegemon. All this has changed with the downturn in the hegemonic cycle. Just as during the British hegemonic downturn of a century ago, the American hegemonic downturn has led to a period of *fin de siècle* forebodings. Erosion of hegemonic leadership is accompanied by loss of universal optimism.

The contemporary shift from social optimism to pessimism is the result of the return of uncertainty. Modernity had been tamed by the hegemonic building of a new type of society, but what is new cannot remain so for long: the American project is beginning to come apart. The turmoil of modernity's incessant change is reappearing to undermine established stabilities and create new insecurities. Enter the debate on globalization (Hirst and Thompson, 1996). This is not a simple culmination of Americanization because there is a crucial difference of expectations. Whereas Americanization was a promise of a better life, globalization operates as a threat. For instance, globalization is commonly experienced as 'downsizing', shedding just those white-collar jobs that once provided for the good life. In terms of their social meaning, therefore, it is better to see Americanization and globalization as opposites reflecting very different times. Globalization as threat is a sign that the American Century as hegemonic cycle is coming to its end.

Epilogue
Presents and Ends

If the reader has reached this far he or she will have realized by now that this book is about past-modernities with little or no reference to current debates concerning post-modernity. This omission is based upon more than the author's personal preferences – I'll write about what I want to – or even the suspicion that a geohistorical perspective may not inform much that goes under the post-modern label. Rather, I follow Berman (1992) in placing post-modern debates into a contemporary historical context so that their content may be viewed as another intellectual attempt to come to terms with the modern maelstrom. In fact, Lash and Friedman (1992, p. 2) interpret this as a three-way debate with post-modernists disputing the claims of 'high modernity' and its abstract universalism while Berman disputes post-modern claims with his popular or 'low modernity', the 'bottom-up' variety. The previous arguments of this book intersect with post-modernity positions in two places. First, post-modernism grew, in part, out of a critique of the modernism movement which in chapter 3 I identified explicitly as not the ordinary modernity I focus upon. Second, post-modernity grew also, in part, out of the idea of the emergence of post-industrial society. This relates to the industrial equals modern equation; if this is accepted then post-industrial means post-modern. But if, as I argued in chapter 1, the original identity is dissolved then there can be a post-industrial modernity as well as a pre-industrial modernity. Hence, despite this final section of the book being about 'presents and ends' it will not engage with post-modernity debates.

In contrast I do take seriously the idea of globalization. Briefly introduced in the previous chapter as a transcendence of Americanization, politically globalization is a very important ideological tool. But it works only because it is based upon real geohistorical processes in terms of trends in communication technology and corporate organization. One important consequence of globalization has been to undermine the credibility of social science disciplines. Economics with its emphasis on 'national' economies, sociology with its concern for societies coterminous with states, and political science with its treatment of politics as government, have each been developed as highly state-centric intellectual projects which have found it difficult to deal with processes that transcend states (Taylor, 1996b). Hence globalization has helped generate a 'crisis of the disciplines', a situation which has created the window of opportunity to develop the geohistorical approach adopted here.

Of course, the crises of intellectual projects is only one among a whole liturgy of identified crises in the contemporary world. This is a time of endings with post-this and post-that – Benko (1997, pp. 9–10) has recently listed twenty-one 'posts' – and I will conclude with a geohistorical interpretation of this widespread foreboding. However, there is an important conundrum for anyone trying to identify fundamental change, in the sense of transition to another world, within modernity. Since the latter is constituted as incessant change, how can perennial adaptive change be distinguished from catastrophic alteration? These are the presents and ends of the title of this discussion. Perhaps here I can learn from the school of thought that has been most concerned with understanding crisis, Marxist historiography. Interpreting crisis as a basic turning point in the development of a mode of production, Marxists have treated the crisis of capitalism in two distinct ways (O'Connor, 1987). First, they have identified inherent contradictions in the development of capitalism which will inevitably culminate in its future demise. This capital-logic approach can degenerate into a 'history is on our side' complacency. Second, to counter political apathy, the class conflict approach identifies the need for political mobilization in a situation where there are changing balances in political power. The end of capitalism is not doubted but it is not inevitably succeeded by socialism. This crude characterization of Marxist positions does provide a simple but useful framework for approaching the conundrum of modernity change. System change and political practice will be used to consider the present state and future of modernity.

System logic: the extraordinary effect of ordinary modernity

In his work on the world between the fourteenth and eighteenth centuries, Fernand Braudel (1981, p. 31) analysed the everyday lives of the population to provide 'an evaluation of the limits of what was possible in the pre-industrial world'. It is in this spirit that I consider ordinary modernity as defining the measure of what is possible in the modern world. The coterie of processes constituting world hegemony and ordinary modernity have imposed a critical influence on the overall trajectory of the modern world-system. For the first time in its history the idea of social limits has seriously entered the collective consciousness of the modern world.

The idea of limits to progressive social change is anathema to the whole notion of being modern. Being defined as subjects rather than objects of social change has required the expectation of a better world in the future. And this social cultural edifice is supremely consonant with the political economy imperative of ceaseless capital accumulation. The capitalist world-economy requires continual economic expansion to survive; every periodic slowdown in economic growth creates a problem of realization or recession which may develop into a crisis of the system or depression. The new political economies created by the hegemons are the major restructurings that have resolved past systemic crises. But the problem will never go away. In a very real sense capitalism *is* economic growth, it cannot stop. The question arises, therefore, whether the Earth is ultimately too small for capitalism.

Modernity is crucially implicated in this capitalist route to ecological disaster. The cultural appeal of becoming modern – which today means ever new consumptions – is what creates the market demand enabling ceaseless capital accumulation to continue. Let me illustrate this with two remarkable examples. In the 'Baby Milk Scandal' of the third world which is now over two decades old, mothers were persuaded, relatively easily, to part with very large proportions of their family incomes to replace breast milk with powder milk formulas (Chetley, 1979). The difference between the two sources of milk is that the former is traditional, free and good for babies whereas the latter is modern, expensive and, in third world water supply conditions, is often lethal for babies. Despite these limitations, it was found that an advertising campaign with nurses dressed up in modern uniforms ensured large sales of powdered milk and consequent rises in infant mortality. They were not, of course, just selling milk; what was on offer here is nothing less than an invitation to join the modern world. And whatever the costs, in both monetary and human terms, it seems that nothing would stop many young women accepting the invitation: it was an offer they couldn't refuse.

My other example of the irresistible seductiveness of consumer modernity comes from communist China. At present its cities operate largely through a mixed system of private bicycles and mass public transport. For large cities, this is a very efficient and low pollution solution to the traffic problem in comparison to Western cities swamped by cars. In fact, one of the ironies of this example is that most city planners in the West promote bicycle travel and predict a necessary return to mass transit in the wake of unacceptable car pollution and gridlocks. Nevertheless, the communist government in China is pushing for the conversion of its many cities into car cities. This bourgeois individualism is central to its catching up with the West. By 2010 it plans to be the third largest car-maker in the world, with 40 million cars on its streets (R. Smith, 1997, p. 44). Of course, this is just a start: to finally catch up with the USA will require another tenfold increase in cars but China is now on a trajectory to that end. This example of Americanization, adding another billion ordinary shoppers to the great mall that is the world market, shows both a political failure to see other than an American future and the absurdity of it all for the future of the Earth as a healthy habitat for humanity (Zhao, 1997). Quite simply, ordinary modernity culminating in American levels of consumption leads to an extraordinary crisis.

Popular concern for the future of the world as the home of

humanity coincided with the beginning of the US hegemonic down-turn (*c.*1970). Books with names like *The Population Bomb* (Ehrlich, 1972) started a debate on the need to reduce population growth. But this demographic debate has become rather stale and predict-able. Pessimists argue that there is no sustainable way forward, optimists believe that technology, or, rather, humanity's inherent capacity to solve problems through technical innovation, will come to the rescue. That, after all, is what progress and development have been all about: devising new technologies to solve problems as they arise. In the 'race' between technology and population, optimists are sure the former will ultimately win and save the world. But such quintessentially modern arguments are weak because they are divorced from the political economy that is capitalism. There is no race. Technology cannot be an exogenous variable; it is socially created and therefore part of the system. Technology and growth are intrinsically linked together in the capitalist world-economy. That is, after all, one of the bases of world hegemonic cycles. The prime role of technology in the modern world-system is to create new products for new markets – for suburban shoppers, for gener-als, for doctors, for businesses, for farmers, for bankers – which is precisely the growth that is relentlessly leading to ecological dis-aster. Modern technology is imbued in the culture of the capitalist world-economy and therefore is part of the problem not the sol-ution.

Superficially this argument seems to come down on the side of the pessimists although with a twist: there is a 'population prob-lem' developing today that is threatening the earth but it is not demographic, it is the increasing population of shopping malls across the world. But it is somewhat more sophisticated than that. It is not only that mass consumption is harmful to the Earth but that this represents a long-term systemic development which has been termed ordinary modernity. 'Consumer society' represents much more than an artefact of the USA, the contemporary face of cap-italism: rather, it is the culmination of a prime tradition of mod-ernity intimately linked to world hegemony. Thus Americanization's popularity based upon its appeal to ordinary people is not totally an invention of the twentieth century. Through the auspices of world hegemonies this cultural trait has grown over four hundred years to dominate the contemporary world as Americanization. The culmination of this process is a world divided into a zone of comfort where most people lead the 'good life' – Galbraith's (1958) 'affluent society' – and a zone of struggle where most people aspire to live the good life. The genie, as it were, has been let out of the bottle: ordinary people can lead comfortable lives. And this is why ordinary modernity results in the extraordinary impasse which threatens the future sustainability of the Earth as a living planet.

But the above argument transcends optimism and pessimism for the world's future. The threat to our planet is not, as the original authors of *The Limits to Growth* (Meadows et al., 1974) described it in their book's subtitle, 'the predicament of mankind'. It is modernity's predicament (no more modern world-system) or capitalism's predicament (no more capitalist world-economy) but humanity need not be that limited in its future choices to this one system with two names. World population is expected to peak somewhere between 10 and 14 billion people in the twenty-first century. There are no doubt many social arrangements which can accommodate this number of people on the Earth's surface but modern capitalism is not one of them. I am, therefore, both pessimistic and optimistic – optimistic for the future of humanity while being pessimistic for the future of the current modern world-system.

Political practice: the post-traditional challenge

'There is a need', according to David Morley and Kevin Robins (1993, p. 5), 'to be "at home" in the new and disorientating global space.' Put in geohistorical terms, how can this global space be prevented from overwhelming the global as place? Of course, the global is already interpreted in both place and space terms. Globalization describes contemporary processes which treat the world as a single space of action. Robert Cox (1996) has suggested the term 'globality' to describe the environmental concern to treat the Earth as a place or single ecosystem. This sets up a classic place–space tension between what Dennis Cosgrove (1994) has called '*One-world*' and '*Whole-earth*'.

The first point to make about this tension is that the two global discourses have remained largely separate, paying little more than lip service to each other's existence. I take it as axiomatic that post-modern, meaning literally what comes next, should not be historically realized as post-life; thus it is essential that these two ways of treating the global need to begin informing each other. This can begin with the basic questions; for a place, what is its meaning? for a space, what is its function? The meaning of whole-Earth place is eco-social security, preserving the web of life. The function of one-world space is techno-social freedom, increasing human progress. How can these be made compatible? Social change cannot be stopped but it can be designed so that it is not self-defeating through destroying life. But this must be more than another plea for good global stewardship: what is the practical politics which might lead to this end?

Probably the most common answer to this political need is to posit some red–green alliance. The relationship between socialists and environmentalists has been a difficult meeting of radical minds for reasons given in chapter 5. This has translated into conflict of the 'jobs versus environment' variety. However, such conflict is a luxury to be enjoyed only within the richer countries of the world. Since the environmental movement originated in the latter, it was only with the globalization of the movement that such conflict could be transcended. This can be dated to the 1972 Stockholm conference which was called in response to European concern for the trans-boundary nature of pollution, especially acid rain. As a UN conference, however, it was subject to a third world majority in the General Assembly who were concerned for the anti-development implications of much environmentalist writing. Were the North saying that now they were developed, the rest of the world would have to forgo their development to save the planet? This was the nettle the environmentalists had to grasp at Stockholm and afterwards, resulting in the invention of the concept of 'sustainable development', a classic 'have your cake and eat it' formulation. Quite simply, 'social justice' was an issue that would not disappear. The fact that America has brought the system to its limits does not mean that social polarization, so obvious in the great nineteenth-century cities of British industrialization, has been overcome. As previously argued, partial amelioration in 'affluent societies' in a limited number of countries is not an answer to the social question at the global level. Hence the radical attraction of something which would be an environmental-socialist movement to confront simultaneously ever-increasing material inequalities within the system and ever-nearer material limits of the system. However, despite three decades of activism on world poverty and world ecology, such a positive politics remains a dream, and one that has none of the popular potency of the American Dream. Perhaps in searching for a new practical politics, combining two old movements is not really the way to a totally fresh political process.

The work of Ulrich Beck (1992; 1994) may provide a way forward here. In chapter 1 his ideas on the modernization of modernity were introduced and two relevant points arise from that argument. First, the politics emanating from a crisis is inevitably a politics of the old modernity. This is because the crisis itself derives from the old modernity and therefore stimulates a political agenda in old modernity terms. Second, and related to the first point, Beck defines modernizations as separate from crises, they are symptoms of success rather than disaster. This is, of course, very provocative; in some sense it counters active political movements towards positive change. But does change have to operate through modern movements? Certainly, in a politics to transcend modernity, modern political movements may well be irredeemably old-fashioned.

What of Beck's (1994) concept of a sub-politics, power games operating in new arenas to new ends, surreptitiously and slowly creating revolutionary change? I illustrated this in chapter 1 by using Beck's example of the changing role of women in modern society which has profoundly affected homes, employment and services. The feminist movement was important in placing the position of women on the public agenda but as a political movement its formal political successes have been limited. Beck would argue that basic changes in gender relations relate at least as much to millions of individual assertions of power, in particular the refusal to be 'captive wives' by remaining in the labour market after marriage. Of course, as well as providing a new independence for women, this new arrangement leading to the two-income household was entirely consonant with consumer modernity, indeed it has been a critical component in sustaining the latter. In other words this was radical change ultimately pushing at an open door because it constituted an important element of the current trajectory of new modern change. The problem with such sub-politics is that they are much easier to identify in hindsight, their very nature making them obscure to contemporary eyes.

Beck (1994) interprets recent sub-politics as creating a new reflexive modernity. This is a social order where authority is perennially under scrutiny. In this era of reflexivity all forms of hierarchy are routinely challenged. The professions whose status depends upon a hierarchy of knowledge are obvious victims of reflexivity. As patients, students, litigants, parents or householders, however individuals meet professionals, they have the consumer movement in all its many guises to promote equality in such transactions. Traditionally, professional associations have protected their members by legitimating their practice as purveyors of specialized knowledge. Against a new assertive public, the simple unequal division of power between provider of knowledge and receiver of knowledge is no longer acceptable. Today the receivers are much less likely to accept the role of being the mere object in this knowledge exercise. Rather, they demand to be the subject, to have their say in the application of the knowledge to themselves.

Beck (Beck, Giddens and Lash, 1994) and others have developed such observations to identify a new reflexive modernity recently superseding 'industrial modernity'. From the geohistorical perspective adopted here, industrial modernity has long since been superseded by consumer modernity and reflexivity looks very much like a development of the latter rather than a new distinct form of modernity. However, Beck's analysis, as developed by Anthony Giddens (1994; 1995), generates the idea of a post-traditional society which provides a particularly fruitful addition to the geohistory presented here.

At first sight it seems odd to describe the latest modern society as post-traditional, because all modernities claim to have superseded tradition. Giddens (1995, p. 57), however, argues otherwise. Although I argued in the Prologue that it is usual to think in terms of modern and traditional as opposites, modern societies have been great 'inventors of tradition'; no sooner is one tradition eliminated than another is found necessary as part of the matrix of social order (Hobsbawm and Ranger, 1983). It is the inability to invent new traditions that marks the present time and makes it post-traditional. This is due to two contemporary social forces. First, the enhanced social reflexivity has led to more and more individuals making decisions about their lives on the basis of considered reflection on options. Second, globalization means that different traditions are facing one another throughout the world on an everyday basis. In combination, these forces have produced 'a world of interrogation and dialogue' in which traditions, whose truth is taken for granted, simply cannot cope (Giddens, 1994, p. 85). For existing traditions the whole context of their existence has changed and a new term has had to be coined to describe their dilemma: traditional assertion of ritual truth is now called fundamentalism whether proclaimed by Islamic mullahs or American patriots. The common fundamentalist reaction to these effects of reflexive modernization has been to look inwards and demand purity while reacting violently to the outside, the new global society.

But if there can be no more traditions, can modernity survive? In the past the prime modernities have defined themselves in opposition to specific traditional worlds: mercantile modernity contrasted with the traditional aristocratic *ancien régime*, industrial modernity contrasted with traditional rural backwardness, and consumer modernity contrasted with traditional third world underdevelopment. In post-traditional conditions modernity is bereft of its cultural 'partner', which Giddens (1994, p. 10) believes will undermine social reproduction. Is this the opening for a new non-state sub-politics? Initially, reflexivity is consonant with consumerism, as in the rise of 'consumer rights'. Perhaps the most important feature of the environmental movement is not its political successes or failures, but its sub-politics, the way in which it has changed the behaviours of millions of people. Healthy eating and keeping fit, rejecting both fast foods and motor cars, can change the face of the world. Are these imperceptible small changes the birth pangs of a new non-modern world?

References

Agnew, J. 1987: *Place and Politics*. London: Allen and Unwin.

Allen, P. 1992: *The Atlas of Atlases*. New York: Abrams.

Allen, W. 1958: *The English Novel*. London: Penguin.

Anderson, B. 1983: *Imagined Communities*. London: Verso.

Archetti, E. P. 1996: Modernity. In A. and J. Kuper (eds) *The Social Science Encyclopedia* (2nd edn). London: Routledge.

Aron, R. 1959: From France. In F. M. Joseph (1959).

Arrighi, G. 1990: The three hegemonies of historical capitalism. *Review*, 13, 365–408.

Arrighi, G. 1994: *The Long Twentieth Century*. London: Verso.

Bahro, R. 1986: Statement on my resignation from the Greens. In R. Bahro, *Building the Green Movement*. London: GMP.

Barzini, L. 1959: From Italy. In F. M. Joseph (1959).

Bauman, Z. 1989: *Modernity and the Holocaust*. Cambridge: Polity Press.

Bauman, Z. 1991: *Modernity and Ambivalence*. Cambridge: Polity Press.

Beck, U. 1992: *Risk Society: Towards a New Modernity*. London: Sage.

Beck, U. 1994: The reinvention of politics: towards a theory of reflexive modernization. In U. Beck, A. Giddens and S. Lash (1994).

Beck, U., Giddens, A. and Lash, S. 1994: *Reflexive Modernization*. Cambridge: Polity Press.

Benko, G. 1997: Introduction: modernity, postmodernity and the social sciences. In G. Benko (ed.) *Space and Social Theory: Interpreting Modernity and Postmodernity*. Oxford: Blackwell.

Berman, M. 1988: *All that is Solid Melts into Air: the Experience of*

Modernity. New York: Penguin.

Berman, M. 1992: Why modernism still matters. In S. Lash and J. Friedman (eds) *Modernity and Identity*. Oxford: Blackwell.

Billig, M. 1995: *Banal Nationalism*. London: Sage.

Billington, J. H. 1980: *Fire in the Minds of Men*. London: Temple Smith.

Blaut, J. 1987: Diffusionism: a uniformitarian critique. *Annals, Association of American Geographers*, 77, 30–47.

Blaut, J. 1993: *The Colonizer's Model of the World*. New York: Guilford.

Blondel. J. 1978: *Political Parties*. London: Wildwood House.

Boogman, J. C. 1978: The raison d'état politician Johan de Witt. *Low Countries Yearbook*, 1978, 55–78.

Bookchin, M. 1995: *From Urbanization to Cities*. London: Cassell.

Braudel, F. 1980: *On History*. London: Weidenfeld and Nicholson.

Braudel, F. 1981: *The Structures of Everyday Life*. London: Collins.

Braudel, F. 1984: *The Perspective of the World*. London: Collins.

Briggs, A. 1963: *Victorian Cities*. London: Penguin.

Briggs, A. 1988: *Victorian Things*. London: Batsford.

Brogan, D. W. 1959: From England. In F. M. Joseph (1959).

Broughton, M. 1959: From South Africa. In F. M. Joseph (1959).

Browning, D. C. 1986: *Roget's Thesaurus*. London: Chancellor Press.

Brucan, S. 1981: The strategy of development in Eastern Europe. *Review*, 5, 95–112.

Bull, H. and Watson, A. 1984: *The Expansion of International Society*. Oxford: Clarendon.

Cantor, N. F. 1991: *Inventing the Middle Ages*. New York: Quill.

Carr, E. H. 1961: *What is History?* London: Penguin.

Carson, R. 1962: *Silent Spring*. London: Penguin.

Castrence, P. S. 1959: From the Philippines. In F. M. Joseph (1959).

Chase-Dunn, C. 1981: Interstate system and capitalist world-economy: one logic or two? In W. L. Hollist and J. N. Rosenau (eds) *World System Structure*. Beverly Hills, CA: Sage.

Chetley, J. 1979: *The Baby Milk Scandal*. London: War on Want.

Chomsky, N. and Herman, E. S. 1979: *The Washington Connection and Third World Fascism*. Boston: South End Press.

City Region Campaign (1996) *Building a New Britain*. London: City Region Campaign.

Clarke, I. F. 1979: *The Pattern of Expectation, 1644–2001*. London: Cape.

Colley, L. 1992: *Britons*. London: Pimlico.

Coplin, W. D. 1968: International law and assumptions about the state system. In R. Falk and W. F. Hanreider (eds) *International Law and Organization*. Philadelphia: Lippincott.

Cosgrove, D. 1994: Contested global visions: *One-world, Whole-earth,* and the Apollo space photographs. *Annals, Association of American Geographers*, 84, 270–94.

Cox, R. W. 1996: A perspective on globalization. In J. H. Mittelman (ed.) *Globalization: Critical Reflections*. Boulder, CO: Lynne Rienner.

Davidson, B. 1992: *The Black Man's Burden*. New York: Times Books.

DeBres, K. 1986: George Renner and the great map scandal of 1942. *Political Geography Quarterly*, 5, 385–94.

Duignan, P. and Gann, L. H. 1992: *The Rebirth of the West. The Americanization of the Democratic World, 1945–1958*. Oxford: Blackwell.

Duverger, M. 1954: *Political Parties*. London: Methuen.

Dyson, K. H. F. 1980: *The State Tradition in Western Europe*. Oxford: Robertson.

East, R. and Joseph, T. (eds) 1994: *Cassell Dictionary of Modern Politics*. London: Cassell.

Ehrlich, P. 1968: *The Population Bomb*. London: Pan.

Elliot, J. H. 1989: *Spain and Empire, 1500–1700*. New Haven: Yale University Press.

Ellwood, D. W. 1992: *Rebuilding Europe: Western Europe, America and Postwar Reconstruction*. London: Longman.

Fernbach, D. 1973: Introduction. In K. Marx *The Revolutions of 1848. Political Writings, Volume 1*. London: Penguin and New Left Review.

Fishman, R. 1987: *Bourgeois Utopias. The Rise and Fall of Suburbia*. New York: Basic.

FitzGibbon, C. 1969: *Denazification*. London: Michael Joseph.

Foucault, M. 1980: *Power/Knowledge*. New York: Pantheon.

Fox, R. W. and Lears, T. J. J. 1983: Introduction. In R. W. Fox and T. J. J. Lears (eds) *The Culture of Consumption*. New York: Pantheon Books.

Freymond, J. 1959: From Switzerland. In F. M. Joseph (1959).

Fuchs, R. H. 1978: *Dutch Painting*. London: Thames and Hudson.

Galbraith, J. K. 1958: *The Affluent Society*. London: Penguin.

Gans, H. J. 1967: *The Levittowners*. London: Penguin.

Gavron, H. 1966: *The Captive Wife*. London: Routledge & Kegan Paul.

Giddens, A. 1990: *The Consequences of Modernity*. Cambridge: Polity Press.

Giddens, A. 1994: *Beyond Left and Right*. Cambridge: Polity Press.

Giddens, A. 1995: Living in a post-traditional society. In U. Beck, A Giddens and S. Lash *Reflexive Modernization*. Cambridge: Polity Press.

Goldman, M. I. 1972: *The Spoils of Progress: Environmental pollution in the Soviet Union*. Cambridge, Ma: MIT Press.

Gombrich, E. H. 1989: *The Story of Art*. Oxford: Phaidon.

Gorz, A. 1994: *Capitalism. Socialism. Ecology*. London: Verso.

Gottmann, J. 1973: *The Significance of Territory*. Charlottesville, VA: University of Virginia Press.

Gregory, D. 1994: *Geographical Imaginations*. Oxford: Blackwell.

Gross, L. 1968: The Peace of Westphalia, 1648–1948. In R. A. Falk and F. W. Hanrieder (eds) *International Law and Organization*. Philadelphia: Lippincott.

Hall, P. 1988: *Cities of Tomorrow*. Oxford: Blackwell.

Hall, S. 1992: Introduction. In S. Hall and B. Gieben (eds) *Formations of Modernity*. Cambridge: Polity Press.

Halle, D. 1984: *America's Working Man*. Chicago: Chicago University Press.

Hartshorne, R. 1936: Suggestions on the terminology of political boundaries. *Annals, Association of American Geographers*, 26, 56–7.

Harvey, D. 1989: *The Condition of Postmodernity*. Oxford: Blackwell.

Hayden, D. 1981: *The Grand Domestic Revolution*. Cambridge, MA: MIT Press.

Held, D. (ed.) 1984: *States and Societies*. Oxford: Robertson.

Helin, R. A. 1967: The volatile administrative map of Rumania. *Annals, Association of American Geographers*, 57, 481–502.

Herz, J. H. 1976: *The Nation-State and the Crisis of World Politics*. New York: McKay.

Hinsley, F. H. 1982: The rise and fall of the modern international system. *Review of International Studies*, 8, 1–8.

Hirst, P. and Thompson, G. 1996: *Globalization in Question*. Cambridge: Polity Press.

Hoare, Q. and Smith, G. N. (eds) 1971: *Selections from the Prison Notebooks of Antonio Gramsci*. London: Lawrence and Wishart.

Hobsbawm, E. and Ranger, T. (eds) 1983: *The Invention of Tradition*. Cambridge: Cambridge University Press.

Hoffman, P. 1962: *World without Want*. London: Chatto and Windus.

Hogan, M. J. 1987: *The Marshall Plan. America, Britain and the Reconstruction of Western Europe, 1947–1952*. Cambridge: Cambridge University Press.

Holsti, K. J. 1991: *Peace and War: Armed Conflicts and International Order, 1648–1989*. Cambridge: Cambridge University Press.

Honey, R. 1981: Alternative approaches to local government change. In A. D. Burnett and P. J. Taylor (eds) *Political Studies from Spatial Perspectives*. New York: Wiley.

Hufton, O. 1995: *The Prospect before Her*. London: Fontana.

Hughes, R. 1991: *The Shock of the New*. London: Thames and Hudson.

Huizinga, J. H. 1968: *Dutch Civilization in the Seventeenth Century and Other Essays*. London: Collins.

Inkeles, A. and Smith, D. H. 1974: *Becoming Modern*. Cambridge, MA: Harvard University Press.

Israel, J. I. 1982: *The Dutch Republic and the Hispanic World, 1606–1661*. Oxford: Clarendon.

Israel, J. I. 1995: *The Dutch Republic*. Oxford: Oxford University Press.

Jacob, M.C. and Mijnhardt, W. W. (eds) 1992: *The Dutch Republic in the Eighteenth Century*. Ithaca, NY: Cornell University Press.

Jacobs, J. 1961: *The Death and Life of Great American Cities*. New York: Penguin.

James, A. 1984: Sovereignty: ground rule or gibberish? *Review of International Studies*, 10, 1–18.

Johnston, R. J. 1991: *A Question of Place*. Oxford: Blackwell.

Johnston, R. J. 1997: *Geography and Geographers*. London: Arnold.

Joseph, F. M. (ed.) 1959: *As Others See Us. The United States through Foreign Eyes*. Princeton, NJ: Princeton University Press.

Kahr, M. M. 1993: *Dutch Painting in the Seventeenth Century*. New York: Icon Editions.

Kallen, H. M. 1933: Modernism. In E. R. A. Seligman and A. Johnson (eds) *Encyclopaedia of Social Sciences*. New York: Macmillan.

King, A. D. 1995: The times and spaces of modernity (or who needs postmodernism). In M. Featherstone, S. Lash and R. Robertson (eds) *Global Modernities*. London: Sage.

Klein P. W. 1982: Dutch capitalism and the European world-economy. In A. Aymard (ed) *Dutch Capitalism and World Capitalism*. Cambridge: Cambridge University Press.

Kossmann, E. H. 1963: *In Praise of the Dutch Republic*. London: UC Press.

Kuisel, R. F. 1993: *Seducing the French. The Dilemma of Americanization*. Berkeley, CA: University of California Press.

Kumar, K. 1978: *Prophesy and Progress*. London: Penguin.

Lash, S. 1994: Reflexivity and its doubles: structure, aesthetics and community. In U. Beck, A. Giddens and S. Lash (1994).

Lash, S. and Friedman, J. 1992: Introduction: subjectivity and modernity's Other. In S. Lash and J. Friedman (eds) *Modernity and Identity*. Oxford: Blackwell.

Latour. B. 1993: *We Have Never Been Modern*. New York: Harvester Wheatsheaf.

Lears, T. J. J. 1983: From salvation to self-realization: advertising and the therapeutic roots of the consumer culture, 1880–1930. In R. W. Fox and T. J. J. Lears (eds) *The Culture of Consumption*. New York: Pantheon Books.

Lefebvre, H. 1995: *Introduction to Modernity*. London: Verso.

Lerner, D., Coleman, J. S. and Dore, R. P. 1968: Modernization. In D. Sills (ed.) *International Encyclopedia of Social Sciences*. New York: Macmillan.

Levey, M. 1969: *The Dolphin History of Painting. The Seventeenth and Eighteenth Centuries*. London: Thames and Hudson.

Livingstone, D. 1992: *The Geographical Tradition*. Oxford: Blackwell.

Lloyd, A. 1986: *The Illustrated History of the Cinema*. London: Orbis.

Lubis, M. 1959: From Indonesia. In F. M. Joseph (1959).

Luce, H. 1941: *The American Century*. New York: Farrar and Rinehart.

Lukacs, J. 1993: *The End of the Twentieth Century and the End of the Modern Age*. New York: Ticknor and Fields.

Lyon, D. 1994: *Postmodernity*. Buckingham: Open University Press.

Mackenzie, S. and Rose, D. 1983: Industrial change, the domestic economy and home life. In J. Anderson et al. (eds) *Redundant Spaces in Cities and Regions?* London: Academic Press.

Manach, J. 1959: From Cuba. In F. M. Joseph (1959).

Mann, M. 1988: *States, War and Capitalism*. Oxford: Blackwell.

Marias, J. 1959: From Spain. In F. M. Joseph (1959).

Marling, S. 1993: *American Affair. The Americanization of Britain*. London: Boxtree.

Marx, Karl 1954: *Capital*. London: Laurence and Wishart.

Marx, K. 1972: *Critique of the Gotha Programme*. Peking: Foreign Languages Press.

Massey, D. 1993: Power geometry and a progressive sense of place. In J. Bird et al. (eds) *Mapping the Futures*. London: Routledge.

Massey, D. 1994: *Space, Place and Gender*. Cambridge: Polity Press.

McCormick, J. 1995: *The Global Environmental Movement* (2nd edn). Chichester, UK and New York: John Wiley.

Meadows, D. H., Meadows, D. L., Randers, J. and Behrens III, W. W. 1974: *The Limits to Growth*. London: Pan.

Michels, R. 1949: *Political Parties*. Glencoe, Ill.: Free Press.

Morley. D. and Robins, K. 1993: No place like *Heimat*. In E. Carter et al. (eds) *Space and Place. Theories of Identity and Location*. London: Lawrence and Wishart.

Mountjoy, A. B. 1963: *Industrialization and Underdeveloped Countries*. London: Hutchinson.

Mukerji, C. 1983: *From Graven Images*. New York: Columbia University Press.

Nairn, T. 1981: *The Break-up of Britain*. London: New Left Books.

Neumann, S. 1969: Towards a comparative study of political parties. In A. J. Milner (ed.) *Comparative Political Parties*. New York: Crowell.

Ney, J. 1970: *The European Surrender. A Descriptive Study of the American Social and Economic Conquest*. Boston: Little, Brown.

Nussbaum, F. L. 1953: *The Triumph of Science and Reason*. New York: Harper and Row.

O'Connor, J. 1987: *The Meaning of Crisis*. Oxford: Blackwell.

O'Sullivan, N. 1988: The political theory of neo-corporatism. In A. Cox and N. O'Sullivan (eds) *The Corporate State*. Aldershot: Elgar.

Oakley, A. 1974: *Housewife*. London: Penguin.

Osborne, P. 1996: Modernity. In M. Payne (ed.) *A Dictionary of Cultural and Critical Theory*. Oxford: Blackwell.

Poggi, G. 1978: *The Development of the Modern State*. London: Hutchinson.

Poulsen, T. M. 1971: Administration and regional structure in east-central and south-east Europe. In G. W. Hoffman. (ed.) *Eastern Europe*. London: Methuen.

Price, H. B. 1955: *The Marshall Plan and its Meaning*. Ithaca, NY: Cornell University Press.

Price, J. L. 1974: *Culture and Society in the Dutch Republic in the Seventeenth Century*. London: Batsford.

Princen, T. 1994: NGOs: creating a niche in environmental diplomacy. In T. Princen and M. Finger (1994b).

Princen, T. and Finger, M.1994a: Introduction. In T. Princen and M. Finger (1994b).

Princen, T. and Finger, M. 1994b: *Environmental NGOs in World Politics: linking the Local and the Global*. London: Routledge.

Princen, T., Finger, M. and Manno, J. P. 1994: Transliteral linkages. In T. Princen and M. Finger (1994b).

Richards, J. M. 1962: *An Introduction to Modern Architecture*. London: Penguin.

Rokkan, S. 1969: *Citizens, Elections, Parties*. New York: McKay.

Rose, G. 1993: *Feminism and Geography*. Cambridge: Polity Press.

Rosenberg, J. 1990: A non-realist theory of sovereignty? *Millennium*, 19, 249–59.

Rowen, H. H. 1978: *John de Witt*. Princeton, NJ: Princeton University Press.

Rupert, M. 1995: *Producing Hegemony. The Politics of Mass Production and American Global Power*. Cambridge: Cambridge University Press.

Rybczynski, W. 1986: *Home. A Short History of an Idea*. London: Penguin.

Sack, R. D. 1992: *Place, Modernity, and the Consumer's World*. Baltimore: Johns Hopkins University Press.

Santos, B. de S. 1995: *Toward a New Common Sense*. London: Routledge.

Sarc, O. C. 1959: From Turkey. In F. M. Joseph (1959).

Schama, S. 1981: The Enlightenment in the Netherlands. In R. Porter and M. Teich (eds) *The Enlightenment in National Context*. Cambridge: Cambridge University Press.

Schlesinger, A. 1968: 'Foreword' to J.-J. Servan-Schreiber *The American Challenge*. London: Hamish Hamilton.

Schumpeter, J. A. 1942: *Capitalism, Socialism and Democracy*. New York: Harper.

Servan-Schreiber, J.-J. 1968: *The American Challenge*. London: Hamish Hamilton.

Shields, R. 1991: *Places on the Margin*. London: Routledge.

Skinner, Q. 1978: *The Foundation of Modern Political Thought* (vol. 2). Cambridge: Cambridge University Press.

Sklair, L. 1994: Global sociology and global environmental change. In M. Redclift and T. Benton (eds) *Social Theory and the Global Environment*. London: Routledge.

Slater, D. 1996: Geopolitical imaginations across the North-South divide: issues of difference, development and power. *Political Geography*, 15, 360–83.

Smith, R. 1997: Creative destruction: capitalist development and China's destruction, *New Left Review*, 222, 3–42.

Smith, W. D. 1984: The function of commercial centres in the modernisation of European capitalism: Amsterdam as an information exchange in the seventeenth century. *Journal of Economic History*, 44, 985–1005.

Soja, E. 1989: *Postmodern Geographies*. London: Verso.

Soja, E. W. 1996: *Thirdspace*. Oxford: Blackwell.

Strayer, J. R. 1970: *On the Medieval Origins of the Modern State*. Princeton, NJ: Princeton University Press.

Sylvan, D. J. 1987: Did Florence have a foreign policy? Paper presented at the Annual Meeting of the American Political Science Association.

Taylor, J. R. 1982: A little light relief. In D. Robinson (ed.) *Movies of the Fifties*. London: Orbis.

Taylor P. J. 1990: *Britain and the Cold War*. London: Pinter.

Taylor, P. J. 1991: The crisis of the movements: the enabling state as Quisling. *Antipode*, 23, 214–28.

Taylor, P. J. 1992: Contra political geography. *Tijdschrift voor Economische en Sociale Geografie*, 84, 82–90.

Taylor, P. J. 1993a: *Political Geography: World-Economy, Nation-State and Locality*. London: Longman.

Taylor, P. J. 1993b: Ten years that shook the world? The United Provinces as the first hegemonic state. *Sociological Perspectives*, 37, 25–46.

Taylor, P. J. 1994: The state as container: territoriality in the modern world-system. *Progress in Human Geography*, 18, 151–62.

Taylor, P. J. 1996a: *The Way the Modern World Works. World Hegemony to World Impasse*. Chichester: Wiley.

Taylor, P. J. 1996b: Beyond state-embedded knowledge: opening space for social science, *Environment and Planning A*, 28, 1917–28.

Temperley, H. 1976: Anglo-American images. In H. C. Allen and R. Thompson (eds) *Contrast and Connection*. London: Bell.

t'Hart, M. 1989: Cities and statemaking in the Dutch Republic, 1580–1680. *Theory and Society*, 18, 663–87.

Therborn, G. 1995: Routes through/to modernity. In M. Featherstone, S. Lash and R. Robertson (eds) *Global Modernities*. London: Sage.

Thompson, Edward P. 1963: *The Making of the English Working Class*. London: Gollancz.

Thrift, N. 1997: Cities without modernity, cities with magic, *Scottish Geographical Magazine*, 113, 138–49.

Tilly, C. 1975: Reflections on the history of European state-making. In C. Tilly (ed.) *The Formation of Nation States in Western Europe*. Princeton, NJ: Princeton University Press.

Tilly, C. 1985: Connecting domestic and international conflicts, past and present. In U. Luterbacher and M. D. Ward (eds) *Dynamic Models of International Conflict*. Boulder, CO: Lynne Rienner.

Tomlinson, T. B. 1976: *The English Middle Class Novel*. London: Macmillan.

Toulmin, S. 1990: *Cosmopolis: the Hidden Agenda of Modernity*. New York: Free Press.

Tuan, Y.-F. 1977: *Space and Place*. London: Arnold.

Urry, J. 1995: *Consuming Places*. London: Routledge.

Vann Woodward, C. 1991: *The Old World's New World*. New York: Oxford University Press.

Villegas, D. C. 1959: From Mexico. In F. M. Joseph (1959).

Wagner, P. 1994: *A Sociology of Modernity: Liberty and Discipline*. London: Routledge.

Walden, G. 1997: France says no. *Prospect (Observer* taster), 9–13.

Wallerstein, I. 1979: *The Capitalist World-Economy*. Cambridge: Cambridge University Press.

Wallerstein, I. 1983: *Historical Capitalism*. London: Verso.

Wallerstein, I. 1984: *The Politics of the World-Economy*. Cambridge: Cambridge University Press.

Wallerstein, I. et al. 1996: *Open the Social Sciences*. Stanford, CA: Stanford University Press.

Walzer, M. 1992: The new tribalism. *Dissent*, Spring, 164–71.

Watt, I. 1972: *The Rise of the Novel*. London: Penguin.

Wexler, I. 1983: *The Marshall Plan Revisited*. Westport, CT: Greenwood.

Willett, R. 1989: *The Americanization of Germany, 1945–1949*. London: Routledge.

Wolf, E. 1982: *Europe and the Peoples without History*. Berkeley: University of California Press.

Wood, S. M. 1997: Modernity, postmodernity, or capitalism. *Review of International Political Economy*, 4, 539–61.

Woolf, S. 1991: *Napoleon's Integration of Europe*. London: Routledge.

Yates, F. A. 1975: *Astrea*. London: Routledge.

Yearley, S. 1994: Social movements and environmental change. In M. Redclift and T. Benton (eds) *Social Theory and the Global Movement*. London: Routledge.

Yilfan, M. 1959: From Yugoslavia. In F. M. Joseph (1959).

Zahn, P. von 1959: From Germany. In F. M. Joseph (1959).

Zerubavel, Eviatar 1992: *Terra Cognita: the Mental Discovery of America*. New Brunswick, NJ: Rutgers University Press.

Zhao, B. 1997: Consumerism, Confucianism, Communism: making sense of China today. *New Left Review*, 222, 43–59.

Index